Long before Leon Morris achieved i
New Testament scholar, he offered h
communities in South Australia in the trying years of World
War 2. Bush Parson *is a charming and fascinating account of*
Leon's ministry to these people, those whom he calls the 'big-
hearted battlers.' It shows that Morris, in valuing so highly a
small, personal and unimpressive ministry (by worldly standards),
practised the wisdom of the cross as well as teaching the apostolic
preaching of the cross. This book is a testament to the value and
importance of the ongoing work of the BCA.

Brian Rosner, Principal, Ridley College

Many years ago, I gifted a copy of Bush Parson *to my bride when*
she was dealing with a major health issue. My dedication read,
'Dearest Gayelene, may Leon and Mildred Morris' faith and love
encourage and inspire your own faith and love of God as you pass
through this difficult time. Love as ever, John.' Leon and Mildred
Morris' story of faithful service and lives dedicated to God contin-
ues to encourage and inspire! Be inspired, be an Inspirer – read
and gift Bush Parson*!*

John Harrower, President, Bush Church Aid,
and Bishop of Tasmania 2000–2015

For over 100 years Bush Church Aid has worked with the people of remote, rural and regional Australia as they have cared for their communities and brought the extraordinary news of love, forgiveness and eternal salvation through Jesus Christ. This engaging story of Leon and Mildred Morris' ministry in remote South Australia during the tough years of World War 2 exemplifies BCA's commitment to 'grit, gumption and the gospel' and challenges us to similarly give our lives in Christ's service.

Philip Freier, Archbishop of Melbourne and
Anglican Primate of Australia

Bush Parson
Leon Morris

ACORN PRESS

Published by Acorn Press
An imprint of Bible Society Australia
ACN 148 058 306
GPO Box 9874
Sydney NSW 2001
Australia
www.acornpress.net.au | www.biblesociety.org.au

First edition © Leon Lamb Morris, 1995.
This 2019 edition is published with permission of The Leon and Mildred Morris
Foundation, to commemorate the centenary of the Bush Church Aid Society.

 A catalogue record for this
book is available from the
National Library of Australia

ISBN: 978-0-647-51985-1 (ebk)
         978-0-647-53030-6 (pbk)

Scripture quotations are from the King James Version of the Bible.
Colour plate photos courtesy of Bush Church Aid Archives. Used with permission.

Cover design and text layout: Graeme Cogdell.
Cover image: 'View from Pildappa Rock, Eyre Peninsula, South Australia', Ian Beattie,
Alamy Stock Photo, ID PW7ERR. The shallow rock pools in the foreground are known
as gnamma holes, which served as natural water tanks for local indigenous people.
Map: Ian Heywood.

Contents

Preface

It is a long journey from Lithgow to Minnipa to Cambridge and then to Melbourne, but in his heart Leon Morris never moved from where he began.

In March 1938 he applied for service with The Bush Church Aid Society. He was asked for written answers to a number of questions about his education, work history, health and his faith in the Lord Jesus Christ.

In response to the question 'What do you understand by 'personal salvation' and how is it obtained?' he answers:

> Personal salvation is the removal of the sins of the individual through the Blood of the Lamb whereby the individual is justified in God's sight and saved from the punishment he had incurred by his sin. It is obtained when the individual in simple faith accepts Christ as his Saviour and is born of the Spirit.

The clarity and Christ-centred conviction evident in these words sustained Leon in the years he and his wife Mildred served with BCA in outback South Australia. It fuelled his later postgraduate study and saw him become a theological college principal and Australia's most prolific biblical and theological author of the twentieth century.

a glamorous area and it will certainly not feature in any list of important places and important people. But for me, at least, it was a shining example of what ordinary, humble men and women can do in difficult and trying times.

This little book then is one man's tribute to the people of the outback, especially those engaged in humble and unimportant tasks which yet, put together, meant a great deal to their community and their nation. I owe much to them and am grateful.

Leon Morris

1

How I Became a Bush Church Aid Missioner

I have never forgotten my first meeting with Tom Jones.

I didn't really want to meet him at all at that time, but I was young and had been urged to go and see him and I did not know how to get out of it. It was back in 1934. I had graduated in science from the University of Sydney and done my year at Sydney Teachers' College. Now I was qualified academically to be a teacher in the high schools of New South Wales. More, I was under a bond to teach for the Department of Education for five years in consideration of the financial help they had given me to get through the university. I was due to begin my teaching at the commencement of the next academic year. But all my class had been reminded that it was the Depression. There would be no jobs. None of us would be teaching anywhere until some money became available to the government.

What was I to do with the unwanted leisure that stretched out before me? I talked the situation over with my Rector, the Reverend R.B. Robinson, Rector of All Souls Leichhardt. I had been converted during my years of study at Sydney uni and had been a regular worshipper at All Souls. 'Robbie' (though I would not have dared to use such an irreverent abbreviation within miles of my respected leader!) had proved a wonderful friend and helper during my early days as a Christian. I had been a regular visitor to his home and the welcome the family gave me meant more than I can easily say to a rather shy boy from the country, new both to the big city and to the life of a committed Christian. All this meant that it was natural that I should talk things over with 'the boss'.

Robbie knew that I was interested in the Bush Church Aid Society (BCA). There had been a visiting preacher at All Souls, the Reverend Tom Terry, who at the time was the Organising Missioner of BCA. I can still see him standing in the pulpit at All Souls one Sunday in the early 1930s preaching on some words from Ezekiel, 'every thing shall live whither the river cometh' (Ezek 47:9). He was not, I think, a great preacher, but he was a warm-hearted man, very much in earnest. He saw the words of his text as applying physically to the dry land in outback Australia. Nothing could live in the drought. But when the rains came it was different. The waters brought life to the barren country.

And so spiritually. When the rivers of the gospel come, people live. I don't remember much about that sermon. But I do know that it changed my life. As Tom Terry spoke, his words were a veritable call of God to a young science student sitting towards the front on the right-hand side of the church and not too far from the central aisle. From that sermon on I have never doubted that part of God's will for my life was to serve with BCA in the outback.

That meant that sooner or later I would have to leave teaching and study for the ministry. At that time the normal qualification for ordination in the Anglican Church was the Licentiate in Theology of the Australian College of Theology. While this could be done in many places, for a Sydney man it meant a two-year course at Moore Theological College, preceded by a preliminary year in which one learned the rudiments of New Testament Greek and other useful things. The period of training was followed by ordination and the serving of a curacy, after which a young man was qualified to go outback as a BCA missioner. People more wealthy than I could buy their way out of the bond with the education department. But I did not have the money so the period before I could get into BCA stretched out before me like endless time. Five years of teaching, then three years of study, then two years as a curate. Ten years. To a new Bachelor of Science not much short of eternity!

But I could not even start my teaching. I was through Teachers' College and out of a job. I tried to get a post in a private school, but I was competing against my brilliant classmates with their first class honours degrees and what chance did I have with my pass? Even the second class honours men were ahead of me. Looking back I think that while I was at the university I should at least have attempted the honours maths in which I was interested. But at the university I was too scared to try. Whatever exam I was facing I was always convinced that I would probably fail. I had no confidence and to take on the extra work that honours involved

3

would (in my opinion) have surely increased my burden to the extent that I would almost certainly fail. And then I would have let down my family who had made some pretty big sacrifices for me to go to the university.

We were not a rich family. My father ran a small iron foundry in Lithgow, but it was doing badly (eventually the Depression ran it out of business). I could not have studied for a university degree without some form of scholarship and I held myself fortunate to have obtained a Teachers' College scholarship which took care of my university fees and provided me with an allowance of £52 a year ($104). Even in those days this allowance was not exactly princely, and it meant that the family had not only to forego whatever earning capacity I had but in addition to put in some scarce money to keep me studying.

I could not throw that away. So right through my university career I had concentrated on passing and put away all high falutin' ideas like honours. At the end I was just thankful that I had made it. As I say, I think now that I should have gone for that honours course in maths. That was always my best subject and I had a deep interest in it. But fear cut me off and now, a pass graduate, I could not get a job.

Robbie thought that it would be a good idea to put the time to good use by beginning my studies for ordination. I was happy to do that, but how? It cost money to go to Moore College and money I did not have. I could see no way of financing my way through even part of the course. It was out of the question to look to my long-suffering family for the funds I would need. They would have been sympathetic, but the Depression was still going on and on and they were getting no wealthier. Only because my scholarship had taken care of all my university fees and made a little contribution to my living expenses had I been able to go to the university. If there was any such scholarship at Moore College, I knew nothing about it.

So Robbie came up with the suggestion that I go and talk to Tom Jones. 'He's the Organising Missioner of the Bush Church Aid Society,' Robbie said. 'You are called to work in BCA and you have every intention of going out with them as soon as you can. Why not go in and ask whether BCA will help you with your fees at Moore College?' It was not uncommon for BCA to help pay a man's college fees on the understanding that, as soon as he was through with his curacy, he would proceed to work with the Society. But, of course, that meant that, only a couple of years after BCA had finished paying his college fees, he would turn up, bright eyed and bushy tailed, all ready to inflict himself on his first bush parish.

That would be a fine way out of my dilemma. I liked study and was nicely in the groove, having gone on from high school to university to teachers' college. To get stuck into New Testament Greek and all the rest of it before I had forgotten how to study was a most attractive prospect. But BCA would get no return for any investment in me for about seven years after I had finished my course (five years teaching as I worked off my bond to the

Department of Education and two years in a curacy). I knew that the good book says, 'Cast thy bread upon the waters: for thou shalt find it after many days' (Eccl 11:1). But I doubted whether BCA would regard seven years as a fair interpretation of 'many days.' It did not seem to me that, when money was short with them (as it was with everybody else), they would be ready to expend any of it on some depressing student who might (or conceivably might not) come good after seven years. They were surely not as short of students as all that.

So I put this to my mentor. He agreed that there was something in it. I should not build up my hopes too high, and in the end BCA might well turn me down. But again, they might not. At least, he said, it was worth a try. Moreover, I remembered Tom Terry. I had told him of the effect of his sermon on me and he had invited me into his office for a serious talk. He had taken note of my lengthy program but had urged me to keep up my interest in the Society. Even if I could not go out soon, I could become aware of what was being done. I could pray for the workers, read the Society's literature and in general keep the vision before me. The years that seemed interminable to an eighteen-year-old would pass in due course and if I used them well I would be the better for it. Tom Terry had always been a kindly and encouraging person. He had now left BCA, but it would surely do no harm to talk to the new Organising Missioner.

I did not know Tom Jones at all. I knew he was Tom Terry's successor in office and that was about all. But perhaps he would

6

be another Tom Terry? At the least he would be glad to know that there was another BCA man in the pipeline, even if that particular pipe was an uncommonly long one. So, I allowed myself to be talked into making an appointment with Tom Jones. The closer the time came the more apprehensive I became, for I could not think that the proposal I would put before him would sound at all attractive to anyone but myself. Would it not seem that an out-of-work teacher was simply trying to bludge on a Society with limited funds with the main aim of providing for himself in a trying financial situation? But I could not face the prospect of telling Robbie that I had not gone through with it. I don't think there was any other reason for my fronting up to the Reverend Thomas Jones in his office one sunny afternoon.

Tom Jones proved to be a very different proposition from Tom Terry. Neither was what I would call an outgoing personality. But Terry was a friendly man, kindly and transparently ready to help. In time I got to know Tom Jones quite well and I was honoured to be among his friends. I then came to know that he too was friendly, kindly and compassionate. He was a truly great man and accomplished some really extraordinary things. But none of this was obvious. I have never known a man who wore less of his heart on his sleeve. I can still see him sitting in his office on that day when I first met him, a slightly built man, pale faced, a little stooped, seemingly disinterested in anything the world had to offer.

He was certainly disinterested in what I had to offer. I probably did not put it very well. I was nervous and I did not really believe that Tom would take seriously the prospect of paying for my college fees now with the prospect of nothing more than my poor services and that only at a remove of several years. But somehow I stammered it out.

Tom Jones listened. I will say that for him. But he left me in no doubt that I was nothing but a bludger to come to him with a proposition like that. Those were depression days, days when people would try pretty well anything to get a job or some way of supporting themselves. Becoming a theological student was perhaps not everyone's cup of tea but at least it meant a roof over one's head, a bed to sleep in and three meals a day during term time. People without any real spiritual conviction may well have tried it out simply for the present material benefits. Then in due course they could think up some way of avoiding the obligations they had entered into. Tom Jones was polite. But he conveyed to me quite clearly the impression that he had no difficulty in seeing through my proposition, that he discerned that my motives were none of the best, and that he was not going to be taken in by such a specious story. He had to work hard to raise the funds to keep BCA going and he wasn't about to waste the money given by little old widows and poverty-stricken pensioners to keep healthy young louts like me from the necessity of getting a real job.

I am a mild-mannered man and rarely get hopping mad. But that was one day when I did. I had been quite prepared for a refusal, even half expecting one. But not a refusal like the one I got. I went out from Tom Jones's office vowing that I would never have contact with him again until I could say, 'Here I am. Fully qualified to be a BCA missioner, and you don't have to spend a penny to acquire my services.' And I did. BCA never spent a penny on my theological education, nor did the Society do anything to help my ordination. They knew nothing more about me until years later when, as curate in the parish of Campsie, I dropped in at the same office to say to the same man, 'I'm ready to go. Do you want me?'

But we go back to the beginning of 1935. I began that year not as a theological student, but as a part-time labourer in my father's iron foundry (when there was work there!). I enjoyed the hard labour and found it much more varied than might have been expected. But I was not sorry when things looked up in the education department and they started appointing teachers from my year. The first I knew about it was the day I got a telegram telling me that I was to report to the public school at Warren on April 1st. I did not know where Warren was, but it sounded as though it was somewhere fairly remote and my first reaction was to wonder whether one of my more facetious friends was trying to make an April fool out of me. In the end I decided that the telegram was too official. Anyway, the joke was on the education department, for all they were getting was me.

So I went to Warren. The train that went to Warren passed through Lithgow, my home town, at around 2 am. I remember sitting up for the rest of the night opposite a warmly clad character in a leather overcoat who persisted in keeping the carriage window down. My clothing did not compare in warmth with his, but I was too shy to ask him to shut the window.

But I arrived in Warren in due course, somewhat cold, and, I found, completely unexpected. Nobody had informed the people at the school that they were to have a new teacher inflicted on them and they had nowhere to put me. My first classroom was the shelter shed in the playground, where I tried to teach the brighter third grades and the duller fourth.

Warren proved to be a pretty town and a friendly place to live in. I enjoyed my experiences there and among other things found that I liked teaching. But for the purposes of this present chronicle the most important thing was that I used my spare time to learn Greek. There was nobody to teach me, but I had picked up a copy of H.P.V. Nunn's *The Elements of Greek* and I steadily worked my way through it. This is not a good way to learn the beautiful language. I did not possess a key to the exercises so, though I did them faithfully, I did not know whether I was right or wrong. Sometimes I misunderstood a point and I would be five or ten exercises further on before the facts of life compelled me to recognise that I was in error. Then I would retrace my steps and try to find out what my mistake was. That is a good way to get frustrated and waste time, but a bad way to learn a foreign language. However, in a fashion I picked up the rudiments and began my first tentative steps in the Greek New Testament.

Towards the end of the year someone in the education

department belatedly remembered that I was supposed to be a high school teacher. So I found myself transferred to North Newtown Intermediate High School, incidentally just down the street from Moore College. I was there for two years, instructing students in maths and science (and finding out that I am not much good as a high school teacher!).

But in my spare time I gave myself over to theological study. I mentioned earlier that the Licentiate in Theology was a two-year course and I thought I would improve the shining hour by beginning the course. At that time seven subjects were to be done in each of the two parts and there was an eighth that could be done with either part. The diploma could not be tackled subject by subject (as it can these days), but the student had to do the whole of a part at one sitting. If he failed in a subject he repeated the whole part. My habitual fear of failing (reinforced by the fact that I was only a part-time student) led me to defer the swinging subject while I concentrated on the smallest number of obligatory subjects for that first year. Fortunately I managed to do reasonably well and passed the part.

But that meant that in the next year I had to do the second part together with the swinging subject. As my marks in the first part had been high enough for first class, everyone kept urging me to take the two extra subjects required for first class honours. With ten theological subjects and a full-time job it was quite a year.

But in the end I made it and found myself academically qualified for ordination. Now a pleasant surprise awaited me. I have mentioned that I was under a bond to serve with the education department for five years. Given my precarious financial situation I had never looked at the possibility of paying off the bond. I simply did not have the money. Even when pay cheques started to come in as I taught there were bills that had piled up and had to be met. While I was in no real want during my three years of teaching neither was I affluent.

But now Archbishop Mowll decided that he would like to ordain me sooner rather than later and he asked me to find out how much it would cost to pay off my bond. So I made inquiries and found that the Department of Education had an interesting system. When I was first awarded my scholarship, I had signed a document which bound me to the department for three years in consideration of the department's help for two years of study. When I had satisfactorily completed those two years, they had me sign a second bond which tied me to them for five years in consideration of a further two years of help. The result of my three years teaching was that I had worked off the whole of one bond and three-fifths of the other.

Now the Archbishop had a fund to help impoverished candidates for ordination and he was quite ready to use some of it to buy me out of the Department of Education. From one point of view it was a bargain for him. He did not have to pay for my three years of theological education for I had done all the work for the Th.L. at my own expense. From another point of view it was a dubious proposition, for all he got was me! Anyway, he paid up and I was included in the ordination of deacons in

February 1938.

It was arranged that I should serve as curate at Campsie where the Rev. Cecil Short was Rector. He was a great man and one to whom I owe much. Two years assisting Cecil Short taught me a great deal about how to run a parish and about a host of other things, outside matters ecclesiastical as well as among them. He was an all-round man, one with an interest in a wide area of life and able to make a worthwhile contribution in whatever area he took interest. To be Cecil Short's curate was a high privilege.

All this meant that when I next confronted the redoubtable Tom Jones I was in holy orders, well into my curacy and with all the usual qualifications missioners with BCA were required to obtain. So I offered to work with the Society and this time I was accepted. I don't think I mentioned that I had been to see him before, and he certainly did not bring it up. Probably he had not remembered it. Why should he? From his point of view it had been no more than a minor irritation more than three years before.

But I was not quite through with Tom's displeasure. While I was at Campsie I had been furthering my theological studies on my days off. At that time there was little higher theological education available in Australia, so I had availed myself of the provisions of the external department of the University of London. That university made its degrees and diplomas available to people almost anywhere, provided that the local education department agreed to supervise the examinations. The procedure was that the candidate engaged in correspondence with the university to get clear what had to be done. Then in due course he or she entered formally for the examinations, applying not directly to the university, but through the local education department. That department in due course received the exam papers from the University of London, supervised the candidate as he wrote his answers, and posted the written answers to the university.

I had entered for the Preliminary Examination in Divinity, the first step in proceeding to the degree of Bachelor of Divinity. The university had an 'advisory' service for external students, at a fee of course. It turned out to be not much more than a book list, but it was an essential for people like myself, far from the halls of learning. So I had lined up my first examination and was busily studying for it.

But I could not sit for the exam until June 1940 and by then I hoped to be a BCA missioner. I would have to go to the capital city of whatever state I was located in to sit for the examination and that meant vacating my BCA parish briefly. So I mentioned it to Tom Jones and sought his approval.

He didn't like the idea one little bit. To do a B.D. of London, he said, was a full-time business and he did not see how it could be done in any BCA parish he knew of. I would be paid by BCA. It was my duty to earn my salary and get on with the job of being a minister to my people. And so on.

I told him that I did not plan to neglect whatever flock he might entrust me with. I had no intention of taking time off parish duties for my study. That was something I would do in my own time. I hinted delicately that, while the Society had an undeniable claim on my working hours, it had none on what I did outside them. I thought that, while BCA work would be strenuous there would not be the kind of planning for and running of organisations that are so frequent in city parishes. So, while the job would be demanding, I thought I could manage some time for study. I reminded him that I had obtained the Th.L. by studying in my spare time while holding down a full-time job as a school teacher. This, I thought, ought to show that I was capable of doing something with my spare time.

In the end I don't think either of us really convinced the other. But Tom did not absolutely forbid my proceeding with my course and that was what mattered to me. He told me that it was his responsibility to see that I did my job and that he would see that I did it. I did not care how grudgingly he gave his assent as long as it was an assent. Tom was undoubtedly full of misgivings about his latest acquisition. But he was stuck with me.

And that is the way I became a BCA missioner.

2

Beginning Work with Bush Church Aid

In due course Tom Jones notified me that I was appointed to take charge of the parish or mission district of Minnipa. It may be that I was unusually ignorant, but, while I may have heard the name 'Minnipa' as a place where BCA based a missioner, I had no idea what sort of place it was or even where it was. But I speedily found out that Minnipa was a little town in a farming area in the Eyre Peninsula district of South Australia. To get there was an experience in itself, for I had never before been out of New South Wales. In those days one did not even think of travelling by air, of course, so it was a train journey as far as Adelaide. And, as neither I nor BCA had much money, that meant a long journey by second-class rail, sitting up all night for two nights running.

I was quite used to the trains of New South Wales so the journey to the Victorian border was more or less routine. But then I changed to the *Spirit of Progress* and I can still remember being most impressed by both its speed and comfort. Nobody met me at Melbourne, so I spent the day wandering round the streets of this new city and taking in the wonders of the queen city of the South.

Then in the evening on the train again, this time for Adelaide. Again there was nobody to meet me and this time it was more serious, for despite my ignorance of Adelaide, I had to find out how to get to Minnipa and then do it. Tom Jones had told me that the next stage from Adelaide involved an overnight trip on a boat to Port Lincoln. That meant that I had to find the port area, and then discover from which part of the port the boat to Port Lincoln started. The citizens of Adelaide turned out to be very helpful and their answers to my questions in the end took me to the right wharf.

I was interested to discover that the boat on which I was to take the next stage of my odyssey was called the *Minnipa*. Though I had had little knowledge of that name until I was appointed to the township, evidently it had mattered to people in that general area. The ship proved to be very comfortable and we had a good trip across to Port Lincoln. We travelled by night and arrived early in the morning. Among the people I met on board was Mrs Chartier, who turned out to be a regular member of the congregation at Minnipa. Indeed, I discovered that she was the pianist who played the piano at our services. It was a good feeling to be thus making early acquaintance with someone from my parish.

I remember the beauty of the sunrise over the ocean as we sailed along and later of Port Lincoln harbour when we arrived in the early morning. And there to meet me was the Rev. Bob Hallahan who had the parish of Kirton Point. That meant that he looked after the Missions to Seamen in Port Lincoln and also a land area to the north-west of the town. Bob was a great man and one who was to become a close friend in the succeeding years. He looked after me, introduced me to our archdeacon, Archdeacon Snow, and in due course put me on board a rail motor for the last stage on my journey.

From the beautiful little town of Port Lincoln, a railway line runs inland in a general northerly direction. Later it curves back towards the coastline which it reaches at Ceduna. Minnipa, I found, is somewhere near the middle of this line and the mission district of which I was to take charge went for about 15 miles (25 km) on either side of the railway and about 130 miles from north to south (208 km).

The rail car got me to Minnipa in due course and I had my first look at the little town which was to be my centre for the next five years. I was met by a clergyman named Chambers, who had been looking after the parish in the months since the previous priest-in-charge left. I did not know Chambers (and for that matter never did get to know him well; he looked after me for a couple of days before he went on his way and I have never seen him since). He impressed me as a quiet man, one with a good knowledge of farming and of soldiering, and incidentally one who was good with tools, a useful qualification for a bush parson and one which I, alas, lacked.

It was not the only qualification I lacked. I was ignorant of farming. I could scarcely tell wheat from barley or a cultivator from a plough.

When I moved around my new parish the locals had many a laugh at my amateurish ideas and efforts on a farm. But I found the farmers a helpful lot, quite ready to take pity on my ignorance and initiate me to some extent into what goes on on a farm. I recall that once they had me milking a cow and, on another occasion, feeding pigs. They even had me driving a team of horses! In such ways I came to know something of what happened to my daily bread before it became flour and to bacon before it saw a bacon factory. But that was all future.

Chambers had arranged for me to sleep at the Chartier farm for the day or two before he left and vacated the rectory, so I renewed acquaintance with the lady I had met on the boat. I found that the Chartier family was friendly and hospitable; both then and in the days that followed they were good friends and warm supporters of what was done in the church.

After a couple of days Chambers left to go to Ceduna. He and I motored up to Pimbaacla, at the northern extremity of my parish. Perhaps wisely, Chambers insisted on driving. And at Pimbaacla I handed him over to Bert Broadley, the Rector of Ceduna, and started the life of a bush parson on my own. This left me free to make my acquaintance with 'Arriet, the name given by my predecessor to the ten-year-old De Soto sedan which was to be my means of transport throughout my area. So I drove the approximately 60 miles back to Minnipa, which was the longest drive I had ever undertaken. Knowing that when I got to Minnipa I would practically live in a car, I had had a friend give me some instruction in driving before I left Sydney and learned enough to get my licence. But that was all in short stints and I found 60 miles a different proposition. But I reasoned that the sooner I got used to it the better – I'd be doing a lot of it!

Back in the rectory I went over the information that Bill McLeod, my predecessor, had left for me. He was an excellent cartographer and I found myself in possession of a series of hand-drawn maps which covered the whole of my area, with the homes of many parishioners marked. Those maps were to be of a great deal of help to me all the time I was at Minnipa. Bill had also left some notes on the parish which told me of a number of people I should call on, where services were held, and so on.

There was also a balance sheet that purported to give a picture of the finances of the parish. But if Bill had the makings of a great cartographer he would have been well advised to keep away from banking or accountancy. I could not make out where the money had come from or where it was supposed to be going to. I guess it did not matter very much, for in the end there wasn't much money to be accounted for and the system was really very simple. The parish, of course, could not pay its way, which was why it was under the care of BCA. The procedure was that the local people made what contributions they could, the Rector collected the amounts and from time to time sent the total, after expenses had been deducted, to the head office of BCA. That head office sent him a salary cheque (if they had enough money!) and another for travelling expenses. But in those first days I found the parish records puzzling.

There came Saturday and, as my first service on Sunday had been slated for the remotest southern part of the parish, I deemed it wise to go down on that day. I did not want to face making a longish journey into unknown territory on my first Sunday as I looked for the place where the first service would be held. McLeod's notes had mentioned the Murphys at Warramboo as hospitable people, very interested in the church, so I sought them out.

They proved to be all that Bill had said and they cheerfully put me up for the night. Throughout my time in that area they were people I looked to for guidance and support. Mr Murphy proved to be a fountain of wisdom, though the guidance that came from the other members of the family was not always infallible. Their ten-year-old son, for example, assured me that Sydney was a dangerous city to live in – if you went out you were liable to get 'a bottle on the block!' I assured him that I had lived in Sydney for a number of years and had never been assaulted with a bottle on the head or elsewhere. But the lad viewed that statement with great scepticism.

On Sunday morning I set out for my first service which was to be held at a place called Kyancutta. First I had the problem of getting 'Arriet started. It had been a cold night and the De Soto was very stubborn, but in the end the engine fired and I was off. Unfortunately, the engine stopped every now and then but each time I was able to get it going again with the learned procedure of pressing the self-starter until something happened. Fortunately, in Kyancutta there was a wise man who operated a garage and he diagnosed a flooded carburettor. He fixed it up in no time.

Then round to the local hall for my first service in my first parish. Two people only turned up! I was reminded of the words of Jesus, that 'where two or three are met together' in his name he will be with them and we proved it in our little service. Thus I was brought face-to-face immediately with the fact that I was no longer in a populous suburb with a flourishing congregation that could be relied on to turn up at the appointed times. In the outback congregations were always going to be small and with unexpected demands on farms the congregations were going to vary in number. Anyway, it was good to meet the two people and I still have a photograph of my first bush congregation.

In the early afternoon I went on to a place called by some Koongawa and by others Waddikee Rocks – I never did find out which was the right name. It was not exactly a city, for in addition to the scattered farms there were a school and a hall, nothing else. My service was to be in the hall, and when I arrived I nearly missed it. The hall was a little stone edifice set well back from the road and with no habitation visible and no apparent reason for its existence. But presently some people trickled along, only to find that the door was locked and that none of us had a key. Someone went off looking for that valuable object, but one enterprising worshipper found an unlocked window and clambered in. We then found that there had been a dance there the previous night and that nobody had cleaned up afterwards. So the parson and some of the early arrivals for the service set to work to remove the rubbish, sweep the floor and make the place tidy enough for a service of Evening Prayer. About a dozen people came and I found it an inspiring occasion (especially as my second congregation thus numbered six times my first!).

As soon as that service was over I was on my way again, this time headed for Cootra East, where a service was to be held in a farmhouse. On the way the De Soto shuddered to an ominous stop and I found I was out of petrol – the car's previous misdemeanours had swallowed up petrol at a greater rate than I in my innocence had thought possible! But across the paddock I could discern a house, so I wandered over to look for help. I found I was at the home of the Beinke's, the place where the service was to be held. So it was a good place to have a breakdown. These good folk put some petrol in the tank, and welcomed me in for the service, which gave new meaning for me to the biblical reference to 'the church that is in thy house'. Then the Beinkes gave me a meal and sent me on my way for the evening service.

That was at Warramboo, a little town on the railway line some 26 miles away. On the way I discovered that driving in the dark over a narrow, somewhat winding road with patches of loose sand from time to time can be interesting! However, in the end I made it and found that we had 33 people there – the largest congregation ever, so the people told me. There was certainly a wonderful atmosphere. And if the beginning of my first Sunday was somewhat disappointing the end was triumphant.

Not every Sunday was like my first. But the same elements tended to crop up. There were frequent times when the congregation was tiny or even non-existent. There were friendly and helpful people. There could be a sense of exhilaration when for some reason there would be an exceptional service in a given locality. And, while I had depressing moments from time to time, it was heartening to know that BCA was enabling me to bring the ministry to people who otherwise would have had few or no opportunities for worship. I have always been glad that I had the privilege of worshipping with the little congregations in the various centres of the Minnipa Mission.

3

The Minnipa Mission

Being in charge of the Minnipa Mission was very different from being curate of Campsie. I now found myself responsible for spiritual ministrations in a parish which more or less conformed to the geometrical definition of a line, having 'length but not breadth' – well, not much! A railway line ran through the middle of my parish and I was responsible for a section about 130 miles long (210 km). Nearly all my centres were based on railway sidings, though one or two were up to 15 miles (25 km) on either side of the line. That meant doing quite a bit of travel. In 1943 over the Good Friday–Easter period I took services in eight centres and travelled 250 miles (400 km). The people also had to do some travelling – I noticed that there were four families at one service, two of which had had to travel more than ten miles (15 km) to get there.

Getting ready to visit the extremities of my parish was quite a business. In the whole parish there was not one Anglican building of any sort, no church, no hall, no rectory. We held services wherever we could, and I carried with me a cloth designed to change a kitchen table, packing case or anything else of the right size and shape into the Holy Table. I took also a set of communion vessels which were the property of the Minnipa congregation (but which the Minnipa people were happy to have used throughout the district), various items of church ornament, and a box of prayer and hymn books. Despite the difficulties, I found that the ladies in most centres had developed quite a flair for making an unpromising building into a reasonable likeness of a house of worship.

Sometimes in a service there was the spectacle of a whole congregation remaining seated throughout the entire service, prayers, hymns, creed, sermon – everything. It was not that the people were irreverent or obstinate. It was just that they were worshipping in a school and, having accomplished the intricate feat of wedging themselves into desks meant for people of much smaller stature (and less avoirdupois!), they felt that it would be more reverent if they stayed thus immobilised than if they were to alternately wedge themselves into and extricate themselves from those tiny seats of learning.

The railway line that ran through the middle of my parish was very important and indeed it was that line that made the settlement of the whole area possible. Without it there would have been no way of getting the wheat and the wool to market and it was largely on wheat and wool that the area was dependent. There were other farm animals on some farms such as cows and pigs, while most people kept fowls for their eggs. Farms were scattered all over the district, mostly 1,500–2,000 acres (c. 3,700–5000 hectares) in area.

Usually a farm was run by one farmer who might employ

a labourer or two, and, of course, his sons helped as well. Occasionally there was 'share farming'. This meant that one man owned the farm and the machinery, while another did the actual work, receiving a share of the crop as his pay (usually one-third). There seems no reason why this should not have worked out well on some occasions, but most of those I met had complaints. The farmers who owned the land often complained about the laziness and poor farming practices of the share farmers. The share farmers I met usually maintained that the owners failed to supply necessary equipment or to get necessary repairs done to defective farm machinery. The system must have worked somewhere – it seems so sensible. But I cannot recall ever finding it working happily.

At first the question of size did not mean anything to me – that was just how big farms were in that area. But in due course I came to learn that the government of the day was concerned. Contrary to earlier ideas it was now felt that the soil was not fertile enough for people to earn a living on the small farms they were working. In the endeavour to correct this the government instituted a scheme which in effect enabled a farmer to buy up his neighbour and then allowed him to grow the same amount of wheat on his larger farm as one of the two farms had grown before. He could use his extra acreage to run more sheep. In that way, it was thought, there would be less dependence on wheat and more on wool-growing. Farms would be more viable, whereas in their original size too many farmers were going broke. I was not (and am not) competent to say how sound their reasoning was. But certainly quite a few farmers were leaving their land at the time I began my ministry at Minnipa.

The government policy of amalgamating farms was complicated by a lack of rain. In my first year I found that for many farmers last year's harvest did not get past the dream of what might have been. Having no income to start the new farm year they were unable to stand the expense of putting a new crop in and they abandoned their farms. A bad season was complicated by other factors: low prices for farm products, high wages in munitions factories, the desire to live near relations when the man of the home had gone off to the war, debts and the impossibility of reducing them under present conditions, transfers of people like school teachers and bank managers. The result of all this kind of thing was that the population of my area was halved in the first couple of years I was there.

In my first year then I lost a considerable number of parishioners who sold up and left. This, of course, added to the problems of ministering to a smallish number of people scattered over a considerable area. There was still the same area to be covered, but fewer people to do what was necessary to keep the church going. And the addition a little later of new areas meant that I perhaps had much the same number of people to minister to, but they were spread over a wider area. There was accordingly more travelling and more expense.

Every few miles along the railway line there was a siding. Sometimes a siding was just that, a siding where trucks could be shunted to leave supplies and to pick up the produce of the farms.

Round others little townships had sprung up and these became the centres of social life for the surrounding regions. In such townships people did their shopping, posted their letters, collected their mail, did their banking and so on. I could never work out why some sidings had townships attached and some did not. Probably distance from other centres had something to do with it. In the area allotted to the Minnipa Mission there were about 20 centres, but they varied a good deal.

We should not think of a township as anything like a metropolitan suburb, or even like a big country town. At Yantanabie, for example, I found two general stores, a school, three cottages for railway workers and two houses. Minnipa, my centre, was quite a city by comparison. It boasted of three general stores, a butcher, a baker, a fruiterer (when there was any fruit; at other times the fruit shop approximated to a general store), a bank, a garage, a hotel, a big school (with two teachers!), and about 30 houses. Notable buildings included the Institute (a hall where all public meetings were held), a police station, a Masonic hall and the post office. Minnipa had four well-defined streets and a few others that might have been recognised had there not been so much scrub about. It was not the largest town in the area. That honour belonged to Wudinna, something over 20 miles (30 km) to the south of Minnipa. Wudinna was the centre of local government and the site of the only hospital in our district.

The area was not noted for ecclesiastical buildings. The Anglicans had no buildings whatever, no church, no hall, no rectory, nothing, and this not only in Minnipa itself, but throughout the whole area of the Minnipa Mission. Our people very much wanted to build a church at Minnipa, and despite our general poverty and the many demands made on our community during wartime, I think we might well have done this. We were inspired by a lady in England who sent us a sum of money specifically to go towards the building of a church at Minnipa. Our people started a building fund and had plans for a church drawn up. We found a local builder who was interested in the project. But that was as far as we could go. In its wisdom the Australian government decided that in wartime Australia all efforts must be concentrated on winning the war. So they refused to give permission for church building, at any rate in places like Minnipa. It was to be the task of our successors to build the church of Saint John.

But our need for a church was somehow made known in war-torn England. Many beautiful English churches had been damaged or destroyed in the bombing and we would have thought that the British had enough on their minds in terms of church re-building without giving thought to an obscure little mission district in Australia. But one day I received a letter from Tom Jones saying that the secretary of the Colonial and Continental Church Society in England had been in touch with him. He informed him that the good people of Coventry, whose beautiful cathedral had been destroyed in the bombings, were interested in what we were doing and wanted to show their interest and their concern. So they sent out a stone from the ruins of their cathedral to be built into our church. They also sent an etching which showed the place in the ruins of the Cathedral from which the stone was taken. The subscription read

This piece of stone was part of the Cathedral Church of
St Michael Coventry, destroyed by enemy action
November 14th 1940

IT IS GIVEN TO THE CHURCH OF St JOHN,
MINNIPA, SOUTH AUSTRALIA WITH THE
GREETINGS OF THE PROVOST AND PEOPLE
OF COVENTRY CATHEDRAL

It was very moving to receive this evidence of interest and concern from people who had so many troubles of their own to preoccupy them.

But, as I have said, in my time there were no Anglican buildings in the Minnipa area. The Roman Catholics had a church at Minnipa, and the Methodists had a church at Wudinna. When I first went to the area there was a Church of Christ minister and he, too, had no buildings. In a year or two he moved on and there was no replacement. There were quite a few Lutherans among our farmers, but, like the Anglicans, they had no ecclesiastical buildings in the area. A visiting minister came from time to time and held services where possible, just as the Anglicans did.

After I had been there a little while the Methodists made their Wudinna church available to the Anglicans for services, which meant a good deal to us. And when the station country was added to my district, I went to a church at Tarcoola which was used by any church wishing to hold a service. Church life depended very heavily on public buildings and on hospitality in Christian homes.

Some of my centres were grouped round schools. At Yarrama, for example, where I held a monthly service, there was simply one little school tucked away in the scrub. Nothing else indicated the presence of Yarrama. When I held my monthly service there the parishioners also had the problem of getting adult bodies into desks designed for smallish children (which for some of the larger members of my congregation was quite a feat!). Minnipa had the largest attendance and its congregation averaged 25–30. In the smaller centres congregations tailed away until in some places there was only one family, with the service held in their home.

In the whole of the Minnipa district, as I have pointed out, there was not one Anglican building of any sort. We held our services where we could. This meant using a hall if there was one, or a school, or a private house. Sometimes we worshipped in the open air, though this was not done regularly. Using a hall mostly meant gathering in a place decorated for the most recent dance. The surroundings were rarely a help to worship, but it was wonderful to see how the congregation coped. There was usually a very real atmosphere of worship.

There was a good deal of cooperation between members of different churches and, for example, as I noted earlier, the Methodists at Wudinna were kind enough to let us use their church for our services. But I was surprised to find that people did not often attend the services of other churches when their own did not have a service. There was a Sunday when I could not take services on account of a throat ailment that took my voice away completely. On that Sunday the Methodists had a service in Minnipa and I drove along to attend it; while I could not use my voice there was nothing wrong with my ears! Some time later I heard that a Methodist drove in from his farm 12 miles away and when he turned the corner to·the hall where the service was being held, he saw my van. 'I thought it was our service,' he said to his wife, 'but there is Mr Morris's van. It must be the Anglican service.' So he turned his car round and drove the 12 miles back home! But this was not typical. There was a good deal of cooperation between the denominations.

The distances and the multiplicity of services meant problems. At Minnipa we were able to have a service every two weeks, but elsewhere once a month was the rule. This made it difficult to lay a strong foundation for spiritual life. I found people very ready to support the church, but very reticent in talking about what it meant to have a relationship to Christ. Even those who had really come to know Christ as Saviour found it very difficult to speak about it. But I guess the main thing was the reality of their spiritual experience.

In an area like this one, finance was always going to be a problem. With the large area to be visited and the small congregations there were higher than usual expenses and smaller than usual numbers of people to cover them. For such an area to be viable some such organisation as BCA is a must. In this way the wealthier congregations in the city are able to support the tiny, scattered groups in the country. Which, I guess, is another example of the way the family of Christ works together.

The services were not without humorous interludes. I recall an occasion when we met in a farmhouse. Everyone was anxious to be in the service and for one lady that meant bringing along her ten-month-old daughter: it was that, or miss the service. But during the service the ten-month-old evidently decided that she had had enough of sitting still and began a period of crawling round exploring, much to the distraction of my congregation, especially the more youthful members. The climax came during the sermon, when the little one returned from what had evidently been a successful exploration outside. She had acquired quite a collection of dirt, while a far from clean old matchstick was clenched between baby teeth. She crawled through the doorway, came round to where I was and smiled a roguish smile at the preacher. It was too much for parson and congregation alike!

At the same farmhouse on another occasion a lamb came through the same door, surveyed the spectacle, bleated feebly and departed. On yet another occasion I was taking a service of Holy Communion and while I was devoutly kneeling in prayer a baby who had been put on the floor to look after itself came alongside and then anchored me by sitting on the back of my legs.

We often had to contend with difficulties in running services.

There was the very hot night when we met at a farmhouse. There was, of course, no cooling and we all decided it was too hot to have the service indoors. So we went outside and found a suitable spot. We had no hurricane lamp, nor indeed any light other than bright moonlight. But there was a real spirit of devotion in that gathering.

On another occasion when we met for worship at night in a little school we found that no one had remembered to bring a light. All we had was one torch. So we sang a verse or two of hymns we knew well, shining the torch on the portable organ for the benefit of the organist. Then we passed the torch over to the minister for reading the service and the lessons. Presently we came to the sermon, when we switched it off to save the batteries. It was somewhat unusual, and it must have been a strange experience for the congregation to hear a voice but see no one. But the incident illustrates something of the unusual way in which people sometimes worship in the bush and of the fact that they can draw near to God and find him drawing near to them in whatever circumstances surround their worship.

It would be wrong to convey the impression that all the people were eagerly searching for the things that Christ alone can give, for, apart from a keen minority, they were not. But they were certainly far from being anti-religious. While they would not have put themselves out to secure a ministry in those parts, now that BCA had provided a clergyman to travel their country, they welcomed him and even gave some attention to his message.

And there were those like an old couple living right out in the bush who were quite alone except for a lad working with them. They were too far away from any town to make any but very occasional trips to it. They really enjoyed being on their own in the outback. They always used my coming as the occasion for a lengthy discussion on some Christian topic and I found their contribution fascinating.

Farmers are, of course, hard-working people and this was true of the people in my area. I did, however, hear of one man whose farm was chaotic and who, people told me, was bone lazy. I happened to meet him on one occasion and when we shook hands I was astonished to find that his hand was softer than mine! His children were in terrible condition, dirty, untidy and living too far away from any school to attend one. I was left wondering what future such little kids could possibly have. But this was the only lazy farmer I met.

My lot was among people who worked very hard, often for all too little reward. Wherever I went people tried to help me by explaining what happened on their farms. I cannot say that I ever learned enough to be a farmer myself, but I learned sufficient to be able at least to take a more or less intelligent part in farming conversations. For some reason I found myself interested in pigs, in the varieties the farmers valued and the points they looked for. And when I visited a farmer who raised pigs (not all of them did) I usually had a look at his herd and asked the farmer what were their good and bad points. In this way I was often given a short lecture on the merits of Large Whites or Canadian Berkshires or whatever the farmer happened to be breeding. I read any articles about pigs in periodicals I came across. And on one occasion I was fortunate enough to be visiting a township at the same time as an expert from the government Department of Agriculture. He gave a lecture on pigs and a farmer was kind enough to take me along. I used what knowledge I had been able to pick up in such ways while visiting a farm in another area. I remember commenting on some of the good points of the farmer's pigs. He had just started this area of farming and I was fascinated to hear him tell his wife, 'Mr Morris knows a lot about pigs and he says we have some good ones!'

The lives of the people were greatly affected by the fact that it was wartime. Many of the young men had joined up so that there were many gaps in families. It was standard procedure that when a young man entered the forces the district put on a complimentary social for him. Almost the entire local population would come together to honour him and wish him well. It was a good custom and one which must have meant a great deal to the lads who were leaving us.

Sometimes we experienced reunions. On one occasion a number of young soldiers had leave together. The day the train brought the boys home nearly everyone in Minnipa was at the station to greet them. The railway authorities enlivened proceedings by announcing that the train would be 20 minutes late and then bringing it in ten minutes late. People heard it coming and they were dashing to the station from all directions. Some did their best to seem without haste so went to the station at the pace of a nonchalant stroll. Others threw all pretence to the winds and frankly bolted.

Then there was a great scene with everybody pressing round to shake hands and tell the boys how great it was to have them back even if only for a short time. But most found it difficult to produce words that would be adequate to the occasion. So people generally contented themselves with saying how wonderful it was to see them back. Very quickly the crowd melted away and left the warriors to be with their families.

During the war there were, of course, casualties and sometimes this involved the breaking of the news of a soldier's death to his family. The people saw the parson as the suitable person to do this and called on me if I was within reach. I recall, for example, being called to break the news to a little family twenty-odd miles (32 km) away from Minnipa. But this happened to me less often that it might have because I was doing so much travelling and the breaking of such news had to be done as soon as the information was available. But it did happen, and it was never easy. I can remember such occasions vividly. One good thing was that there were always people to rally round. The community stood by its own.

There was little that our communities could do to support the war effort but what could be done was done. The ladies in Minnipa, for example, had a branch of the Red Cross which was quite active. And the men at Minnipa had a reserve group that trained on Saturdays. I never did find out the exact purpose of the training. Did they expect that paratroopers would drop in on us in Minnipa? Or was it just a gesture of unity with our men in the forces? For whatever reason, the men of Minnipa took their training seriously. I found myself pressed into service to teach the men semaphore, a system of signalling that I remembered from my days as a Wolf Cub.

I had never progressed beyond being a Cub, but I found that there was a troup of Boy Scouts in Minnipa and that I was expected to be scoutmaster. Somewhere I got a book on scouting to find out what was involved and also began studies for the Wood Badge, a course for scoutmasters. With the help of the instruction the boys gave me and that conveyed by books on scouting I somehow managed to do the job. I can still recall being hauled out of bed early in the morning to run a 'Scout mile' with lads learning how to pace themselves (they were required to travel a mile at a steady pace; was it to take 12 minutes?). And to keeping an eye on those who were keen on securing badges for proficiency in one or other of our activities.

Part of the work of a parson anywhere is, of course, the conducting of wedding services. As people generally see marriages as important, we would expect that on such an occasion everything would be carefully prepared. And often this was the case. But sometimes things went haywire.

On my first occasion as the celebrant at a bush wedding in my parish I was working quietly in my study one Saturday evening when I got a telephone call from a little centre about 14 miles away. In effect the young man was saying, 'Will you come down straight away and perform a wedding!' For some reason the happy couple had made arrangements with a clergyman down on the coast to come up to their farm and take the service. According to Anglican custom he should not have agreed to do a service in my parish without consulting me and to this day I have never found out why he had dispensed with this formality.

But he had agreed to come. The people had expected him to be there for an afternoon wedding and when he did not turn up, they waited for quite a while. They were several miles away from a telephone, so in the end one of the family drove to the nearest phone and tried to talk to the minister they were expecting. But the exchange connecting him was one of those that closed down over the weekend. So, they could only conclude that some calamity had overwhelmed the clergyman and that he would not be coming.

All the wedding guests were there. The bride had adorned herself. The wedding breakfast had been prepared and all things were now ready. The only thing missing was the parson! As they could not get the minister with whom they had made the arrangements they decided to try me. I cannot say that I was very thrilled at the prospect of taking my first South Australian wedding under such circumstances, but who could refuse to help in such a situation?

There was a problem that would not have occurred to anyone

in the wedding party, namely that the government regulations that had to be observed and the forms that had to be used varied from state to state. All I knew was how to conduct weddings in New South Wales. So I had to dig out the information and the forms the South Australian authorities had sent me and hope to goodness that I would not make a mistake in hastily using unfamiliar forms or make a legal error that would have untold consequences!

When I arrived at the farmhouse it was a hive of activity. But we managed to get the necessary forms filled in. Then at about 10 pm the service started. By that time some of the young men who had been fortifying themselves with liquid nourishment were quite merry and it was not easy to get attention from everyone. A couple of times I interrupted the ceremony to ask them to be quiet without much success. In the end I stopped and delivered a little homily on the serious nature of marriage and told them all that if there were any more ribald interruptions, I would stop the service and go home. That had the desired effect and we were able to go through to the end without further trouble.

But it was quite a night. It must have been no small strain on the young bride I thought. But later I heard that next morning it was the bridegroom who collapsed! He was a nervous young man and the strain was too much. But his bride was evidently quite unaffected.

I did not take many weddings. Of course, many of the young people from the area were in the services, and when they thought of marriage they not infrequently had the ceremony performed in the city while on leave. The bride could go over to Adelaide a day or two earlier and they saved the precious time that would have been taken up by the bridegroom travelling over to our region. There was one occasion when I was asked to marry a couple and I worked it out that it was just over two years since I had last conducted a marriage service.

But there were some happy occasions. In one of my smaller centres there was a wedding at which everyone in the district was present. In such places the troubles that beset city folk in drawing up a list of those to be invited and sending out formal invitations just do not exist. You just let it be known that you intend to be married and the thing is done! The word is quickly passed round and in due course on the appointed day all the people in the area leave whatever else they would be doing and assemble in the local hall.

On this occasion there was the occasional hitch to be overcome. The parson had three punctures and one blow-out on the way. But in the end even he made it and found everything in readiness. The friends of the bride had been busily engaged, some in preparing the hall to look as much like a church as they could make it, others in preparing a sumptuous repast which was cunningly hidden at the back of the hall. Someone had brought along a very nice piece of carpet which was rolled from the hall right out to the car from which the dainty bride stepped. Thus, she entered the hall and the solemnly beautiful words of the marriage service joined together these two who had known each other from childhood.

The signing of the register was not always a straightforward matter to those who were more used to the plough than the pen. But in due course we surmounted all the obstacles and the joyful bridal party went off for a drive away somewhere while willing hands transformed the hall from the likeness of a church to the likeness of a banqueting hall. Then the happy couple and their attendants returned in style and the wedding breakfast began. The toasts were a merry affair, with many a quip at well-known local personalities. In all innocence I called on the bride's father at one stage of the proceedings, whereat he responded that he had never made a speech in his life and that he thought I understood he had no intention of starting then! But he did his best and a very good best it turned out to be.

Unexpected happenings of a different kind occurred when I was asked to do rather unusual duties. On one occasion I encountered a young man in deep distress – he had taken a correspondence course on playing the banjo-mandolin and found himself completely stumped on the first lesson. 'Could you help me out, Mr Morris?' he asked. Those who know me and are conscious of my musical limitations will find it hard to believe, but after some concentrated study of those lessons I managed triumphantly to play the first line of 'Home, Sweet Home' and show him how it was done!

On another occasion a schoolteacher in a remote spot surprised me by asking, 'Can you cut hair, Mr Morris?' 'I'm afraid I'm a bit like the man who was asked whether he could play the violin,' I replied, 'I don't know, I've never tried!' However, he was in such a desperate plight that he insisted that I have a pop at it. For the next quarter of an hour or so I worked industriously and had cause to marvel at the many things that can happen during a haircut and to regret that I had not taken fuller advantage of waiting periods in various barbers' shops to observe more closely the professional attack on the problem. In the end I had copious quantities of hair on the floor, but concerning the schoolteacher's head, perhaps the least said the better!

Then there was the day when I was visiting a farm, unfortunately without Mildred, my wife. The lady of the farm, somewhat to my amusement, dumped a noisy and rather cranky baby on my lap while she went off to make a cup of tea. Another woman farmer, with perfect disregard for nice distinctions between men's work and women's work, thrust an iron into my hand and gave me peremptory instructions to finish ironing a pillow case when a phone call suddenly interrupted her in that task. Women in the Minnipa Mission did not stand on ceremony.

At other times I found tasks of a more congenial nature. On one farm there was a young man whose ambition was to join the air force. But for the section in which he wanted to enlist a knowledge of mathematics was required and this he did not have. So each month when I came to his area I had a lengthy maths session with him. As I had majored in maths in my science degree that was quite up my alley. What was not was to find myself one day on the board at the back of a combine driving a large team of horses. I have forgotten why the farmer wanted me to do it, but I can remember what a thrill it was to find a team of strong horses pulling at my bidding.

There could be some sad occasions. At around 2.15 am one morning Mildred and I were roused from our slumbers to find that one of our church members was on his way home from the hospital at Wudinna where his wife, one of our active church members, had just died after a sudden illness. Would we come out and stay the rest of the night, if need be, and break the news to the children? We would and we did. Then, of course, came all the arrangements for the funeral which was a sad occasion for the whole district. Everyone in the town felt the loss.

And when the funeral was over one of the mourners claimed Mildred's attention because of the sudden onset of some mysterious illness. Mildred, a nursing sister, did what she could before and during a 60-miles-an-hour dash to hospital, only to find that the doctor was out on an urgent case. However, he returned in time to diagnose pulmonary embolism and proceed with treatment. The woman recovered but the doctor said that had there been a delay of even an hour it would probably have proved fatal. We gave thanks for the St Patrick's Van (for this van see chapter five).

Sometimes in the normal order of things I was asked to conduct baptisms. Fortunately, none of them were in the style of the one in the poem, 'On the outer Barcoo, where the churches are few.' Of course, there was never a font – we generally did our best with a glass dish of some sort placed on a table in front of the congregation. It was the responsibility of the locals to produce such a glass dish and naturally sometimes everybody forgot. At one school I recall that someone found a large vase which might have been made of cut glass (and might not!). Anyway, it served the purpose. Improvisation was a law of life in those parts.

On one occasion in a remote home where there was a large family, I was asked to baptise the youngest. The older ones could remember their own baptisms and what they told the kid I never found out, but it was clearly horrifying. The child was expecting something in the nature of the branding of cattle which he had seen so often. He was greatly relieved when he found out what he was required to undergo.

The Prayer Book says that baptisms should take place 'when the most number of people come together' and this at least was something we did quite literally. As the family was always well-known to all the people who lived in the area nearly the whole population would turn up as a matter of course. Baptism was quite an event for the community as well as for the family.

Harvest thanksgivings were of the greatest importance in these farming communities and they were magnificent occasions throughout the area. I took 17 of them each year and they varied from congregations comprising two families who came together to worship in the commodious kitchen of a farmhouse, to assemblies of most of the local people in the hall that was used for most public functions. For one service in the Methodist Church at Wudinna we had ecclesiastical surroundings. But wherever it was held and however many (or few) people attended, Harvest Thanksgiving meant a great deal to people who made their living from the land.

Here is what happened one year at Pimbaacla. This little city on my northern boundary boasted one shop with dwelling attached (or was it a dwelling with shop attached?) and a school. There was also a wheat shed but that was part of the railway rather than the town. We always worshipped in the school. On this occasion when I turned up I found the usual knot of farming men standing in the shade of a tree and gravely putting to rights the affairs of the world. I always liked this little forum with its leisurely debates and interesting conclusions.

In the school an energetic band of women was putting the final touches on preparations for the harvest festival. They had a stool with a back which they had draped with a sheet and flanked with sheaves of hay and bags of grain. On and about the stool they had arranged as great a variety of farm produce as their combined effort could muster.

In due course the congregation trooped in. Soon all the available seats were occupied amid sundry little pleasantries as the not-so-slim tried to insert themselves into desks obviously designed for those of more tender years (and lesser girth). With all the desks occupied someone remembered another desk or two in the shelter shed, but this was only a partial solution to the problem. Sundry car seats were brought in but these, too, were not enough. Some resourceful person proceeded to dismantle a cupboard which consisted of fruit cases artfully put together and concealed. We placed the cases along a wall, covered them with a rug and behold, a seat good enough for the highest in the land! We sat a row of little girls in front of the desks and thus we were all nicely fitted in. Except that during the singing of the first hymn the inevitable pair of latecomers arrived, and we held up the service while we fitted them in. To add to our difficulties a wretched little dog refused either to stay outside or to keep quiet. But a determined-looking male strode purposefully out, was absent for a few minutes, and we heard the dog no more.

At Pimbaacla we had no musician to accompany the singing and despite my musical limitations I had to start all the un-accompanied singing. Hymns can be a great trial! But our worship at that little service was sincere and from the heart. I have been to Harvest Festivals in more convenient buildings with more varied decorations, with beautiful organs and talented choirs to give a more worthy musical expression to our thanks, with more comfortable surroundings and lower temperatures, with larger congregations and better preachers. But I have never been to one more impressive than this little outback expression of heartful thanksgiving with its simple dignity as men and women who live by the land returned their thanks to the Giver of all for his mercies in the harvest he has given them.

To give every centre a chance to have such a service meant that the thanksgivings went on for a full month. Decorations of wheat and oats or sheaves of hay were standard and not at all surprising. But I was amazed at the variety of fruit and vegetables that adorned our halls and schools for the services. One old bachelor farmer told me that he had nothing suitable he could bring, nor had he money to make an offering, but he asked me whether I would accept two bags of rye as a thank-offering for all God's goodness to him. I was happy to do so, and I subsequently sold them to another farmer for ten shillings ($1) a bag. To this day I do not know whether the second farmer got a bargain or whether I was profiteering. I was in continual surprise at the offerings made at such times. The people were poor, but they made sacrifices to give of their best as thanksgiving to God for his mercies.

4

Teaching the Children

It seems to me that the children are the ones with most to put up
with in the sparsely populated parts of our great continent. True,
they don't seem to worry about it, but it is the case that they suffer
many disadvantages in comparison with their city opposites. They
often grow up without any companions of their own age. Their
primary education is frequently attended by serious difficulties,
such as travelling long distances under the full blaze of the outback
sun, and then stewing all day in a box 15 feet (4.5 m) square
called, for want of a better name, a school. Secondary education
is sometimes impossible and, where possible, it means separation
from home. These difficulties in the secular sphere are paralleled
in the religious, for the education of the children in spiritual matters
is all too frequently neglected.

When I first went to Minnipa I found that, contrary to the
experience I had had in New South Wales, the schools were closed
to ministers of religion. I had been used to receiving lessons from
my minister when I was a boy, and to sitting back and enjoying
a period off when I was a teacher. Then, of course, as a curate I
did my regular stints of taking religious instruction in the schools

of Campsie.

But in South Australia there was nothing of the sort and I missed it. However, in my second year at Minnipa there was a great change. The state government decided to allow ministers of religion to instruct children in the elements of the Christian faith. That opened up a door of opportunity, but at first I thought it was going to be too big a task. I counted up 27 schools in my area. The larger ones (like that at Minnipa) had two teachers and as many as 70 scholars. Others were smaller, mostly with one teacher and the smallest having six students in attendance, the minimum number for a school to keep open.

Of the 27 schools in the area one had not been opened, though it had been in place for months with the potential scholars eagerly waiting for something to happen (well the parents were eager, anyway!). A second was temporarily closed while the education department tried to replace a teacher who had enlisted in the armed forces. In a third the enrolment was one hundred per cent Lutheran and that meant that I was not permitted to instruct the students. That left me with 24 schools in which I could give religious instruction.

I was able to visit each school once a month in my regular parish program. This, of course, was not much, but I was thankful for anything. The ignorance of most kids in matters spiritual had to be seen to be believed. They were, of course, out of reach of any Sunday School and most parents did not feel qualified to instruct their children in religious affairs. So they were left with what they could pick up in the normal course of country life which, I found, was not much.

For example, there was a confirmation candidate I asked to look up a certain text in the Bible she held in her hand. She looked at me blankly so to give her a bit of help I said, 'It's in the New Testament.' She replied, 'What's that?' Or again, when I was entitled to take classes in the schools, I asked a number of times what the students knew about the Good Samaritan. Two pupils volunteered the information that they had 'heard of it', but all the others confessed complete ignorance.

One bright twelve-year-old informed me that she did not know what a Bible was. In several schools I asked those in the highest primary grades how many Gospels there are and what are their names? Nobody knew the answer to the first question and the only reply to the second was one boy's answer 'Luke'. Clearly there was a need for religious instruction. And there were not many religious teachers. Of the 24 schools I visited 19 were unvisited by any other clergy or teachers of religion, so I had 19 schools which were my sole responsibility for religious instruction.

As I could get to each school only once a month, clearly I needed help. So I turned to BCA's Mail Bag Sunday School lessons. These formed a correspondence course and they were intended for use by children who lived in remote parts who could not attend a Sunday School. The children did the lessons at home week by week and posted back to BCA their answers to questions posed to them at the end of each lesson. The Society had enrolled helpers in Sydney (and I guess elsewhere) who marked the questions and helped the students wherever they could.

I did not want to add my 19 schools to an already overburdened system, but I was able to get the Mail Bag Sunday School to send me the lessons I would need for the 190 students all told in my classes. Then when I visited a school, I would go through the first lesson with the children and leave the lessons for the rest of a month with them. For the older children answers were to be written to questions posed by the lessons, while for the younger folk there were activities like colouring a picture or modelling in plasticine. When I next came, a month later, I would collect the lessons and mark them and leave with the children the lessons for the next month. It was probably not ideal, but at least it meant that the children were getting some Christian instruction where previously they had had none.

This formed a means of involving friends back in Sydney and elsewhere. Some interested people sent me crayons, coloured pencils, plasticine and the like, as well as Bibles, New Testaments and Gospels which I could distribute to my pupils. The lessons cost me three shillings (30 cents) per child per school year and some of my friends chose to help with the cost.

One thing that pleased me very much was that the children did not seem to regard religious instruction with its attendant written work as an added burden. When I recalled how I viewed homework in my childhood days I was somewhat surprised and very pleased at the way the lessons were accepted. There were, of course, some boys and girls who did not like it much, some who were indifferent and some who were just plain lazy. But most of the kids enjoyed receiving the printed lessons and doing the work that was associated with them. They knew I was doing this in all my schools and I guess there was a certain amount of pride – our school is better than any other! At any rate I always met smiling faces when I came round after a month's absence and took things a stage further.

There was of course nothing compulsory about the lessons I left to be done before I came back in a month's time. But I found that about four-fifths of all the work set was done. And a lot of it was done well. I promised that there would be prizes for those who did especially good work, and thus at the end of the year I found myself giving 50 prizes for especially good work. And interestingly some of the best work was done by children whose parents had no interest in the Christian church. Perhaps religious studies came to them with all the attraction of novelty!

Some unexpected happenings took place. In one school I had the children of an avowed and somewhat militant atheist. I had had the occasional debate with him when I happened to encounter him while visiting. But now he sent me a ten-shilling note, with the request that it be used to provide Scripture lessons for his children! While most religious people did not do the same at least I think they were very happy that the kids were getting the kind of instruction in the Christian faith that they would have liked to give if only they knew how.

Correspondence lessons were also part of our normal

Leon and Mildred Morris with St Patrick's Van at Tarcoola, Minnipa Mission, 1944.

Leon Morris with a bogged St Patrick's Van at Woomera, c. 1940s.

Road under drifted sand, Minnipa, c. 1940s.

Sand drift, Yarrania, c. 1940s.

Drought in Minnipa, c. 1940s.

Main road through Minnipa Mission, c. 1940s.

In Minnipa Mission, c. 1940s.

*Mother and baby,
Wynella, Minnipa
Mission, c. 1940s.*

Settlers' home at Palabic, near Minnipa, c. 1940s.

Off to Minnipa for school, c. 1940s.

*Minnipa from
the air, c.
1940s.*

Dry salt lake at Yaninee, near Minnipa, c. 1940s.

Leon Morris with Bishop Donald Robinson at the launch of Bush Parson *in Sydney, 1995.*

Leon Morris at the launch of Bush Parson *in Sydney, 1995.*

preparation for confirmation. There were never large classes, of course, but at least I could see all my confirmees individually each month on my rounds. I was able to impress upon them the solemnity and importance of what they were about to do and the necessity for a personal faith in Christ. Then I would leave with them the correspondence lessons and take them up next month when I came round. It was not a perfect system, but at least the candidates got my undivided attention whenever I could get to see them. And, as in the case of the school children, the correspondence lessons helped them to understand the central teachings of Christianity and the importance of personal commitment.

What they lacked was the sense of fellowship that comes from regular attendance in a large class. In our cities, confirmation candidates know what it is to have quite a few others confirmed with them, but in the bush that was never possible. On one visit of the bishop, for example, there were confirmations in three centres: I had one confirmation candidate in each of two centres and six at the third. But at least each of the candidates was in no doubt about the individual attention they all received.

On one occasion two nurses approached me after service and said simply, 'We'd like to be confirmed.' I was glad to hear this, but arranging for their instruction was not straightforward. I used to visit their town once a month but of course I had to visit people in their homes, look up the sick in hospital and do other such things. Moreover, nurses' hours do not always fit in with the needs of wandering parsons, and to complicate matters one was on night duty and one on day duty. But the matron proved helpful in arranging a monthly period when the two could be free together so we got started.

One lesson a month is not ideal, but we were able to use BCA's Mail Bag Sunday School lessons. The set for confirmation provided a useful summary of the church's teaching on each of the more important aspects of the Christian faith and practice. The two nurses took one lesson a week. They read through the notes together and discussed them. They wrote out their answers to the questions provided and produced them for my inspection when I came round. Generally I found that their spiritual keenness had brought them to right ideas on the subject, but where it was necessary I was able to correct an error or right a misapprehension. In the end I think they were as well prepared as most candidates I have seen during my ministry.

Once again I was able to use the Methodist Church at Wudinna. All the church people turned out in force for the occasion, the parents of both candidates being in the congregation. One family lived 60 miles north and the other 80 miles south of Wudinna, so it was not easy for them to be present but they both made it.

The confirmation was the solemn culmination to months of preparation. The centuries-old service, with its emphasis on dedication and the gift of God's Holy Spirit, lived again. And thus two more of God's children entered into the wider fellowship of his church.

The bishop was, of course, always treated as an honoured guest and parishioners were glad to have him visit them or stay with them. Our bishop was a humble man and looked for no special treatment. But even he was somewhat surprised on one occasion when as we journeyed, we had to cook our meal over an open fire. He himself was pressed into service and grilled his sausage on the end of a stick held over the flames, Boy Scout style. I think he enjoyed it as much as we did.

5

Saint Patrick's Van

There is always a problem in working an area like that of the Minnipa Mission, for a good deal of travelling is necessarily involved and that means a lot of time can be wasted. The waste of time would be lessened considerably if there were places where the minister could stay while conducting a visitation at some distance from his main centre. Of course, in the Minnipa Mission there were many farms inhabited by hospitable people. But, while many of our farmers would have been glad to put up the parson for a night, they were unable to do so because their families were large and their space was limited. They were on the whole rather poor people and they were not able to build big and luxurious houses. Their homes usually coped with their families but that was all.

So in my first year at Minnipa I did a good deal of travelling. There was no problem about food. There were no restaurants or fast-food outlets, but farmers' wives could always fit in an extra one at a meal and they were happy to do so. Sometimes this involved unexpected manoeuvres. One day when I was at a farm house at lunch time we were all greatly troubled by flies. For some reason they were there in droves and, of course, the farm did not have fly-proof doors. The lady of the house solved the problem by putting the food, plates, and so on on the table and covering them with the tablecloth! We lifted up our part of the cloth to get at what we wanted underneath. This may have been unorthodox, but it certainly kept the flies away from what we ate.

But such heroic measures could not put the parson up for the night. It was the bed that was the problem.

A further problem at Minnipa was that my vehicle was a car that had seen ten very hard years and it was always likely to give up on me. It would have saved a lot of time if I had had a vehicle that could be relied on to get me where I wanted to go at the time I wanted to be there. Allowing for mechanical breakdown and effecting the necessary repairs if there was one took up a lot of time.

I recall an occasion during my first year when Miss V. Mannett, a missionary of the Church Missionary Society, came to Minnipa as part of her work to tell people what the Society was doing in places overseas. It was a privilege to have her to speak to our people about what was being done to spread the gospel, and we all appreciated her visit.

But I recall that on our way between two services the car came to a sudden stop. I speedily ascertained that the trouble was in the carburettor, but putting it right was another matter. Miss Mannett asked me what the problem was, and I told her it was in the carburettor, but that I was not quite sure how to fix it. 'Let's pray about it,' she suggested. I agreed and she started a prayer with,

'Lord of all carburettors ...' To this day I am not sure what I did right, but presently we were on our way again. It was wonderful to get a speedy answer to her prayer, but it would have been helpful to have a vehicle which did not create such emergencies.

But a change was coming in my second year at Minnipa. At the end of my first year I went back to Sydney to be married and have a honeymoon. Perhaps I should mention that on the way to Adelaide the De Soto broke down four times, so it was far from an uneventful trip! And I was more than glad to find out when I got to Sydney that I would not have to use the old car again. That was such good news that it was almost an extension of the honeymoon!

Tom Jones had been in contact with some good friends in Ireland. In that country, I found out, there were many people who were interested in what the church was doing in the outback parts of Australia. Some of them had written to Tom saying that if it would be useful, they would be glad to donate the money to buy a van for use in some outback ministry. It so happened that both Tom and I were getting fed up with the De Soto and it seemed to Tom that the ideal thing would be to pension that car off and replace it with the van from Ireland.

The Irish made two stipulations: the van must be green, and it was to be called 'St Patrick's Van.' Neither stipulation, of course, bothered either of us in the slightest, and for the rest of my time at Minnipa I went everywhere in the green van with the Irish saint's name. A side effect was that wherever I was not known I found that for some reason people thought I belonged to another denomination! Saint Patrick initiated quite a few interesting conversations.

The van Tom bought was a GMC panel van. It had hinged panels cut in the sides, which could be opened up and propped open with steel rods so that there would be ventilation in the back when the van was used for sleeping. A cupboard had been built in and there was a Dunlopillo mattress cut to fit the area available for sleeping. It proved to be a very comfortable place for our slumbers, though it presented us with the occasional problem. Have you ever tried to make a bed while squatting in the middle of it? It calls for a technique all its own! And when you have made the bed have you tried undressing in a confined space where it is impossible to stand? And in the morning dressing in the same confined space? Such things caused us amusement at first but before too long we evolved the necessary techniques.

Once early on we parked the van on a gentle slope and went through our routine to get to bed, only to find that the gentle slope meant that our heads were lower than our feet. While, of course, some people may well be able to sleep with feet on high we found that we could not. I had to get out of bed and drive the van around until we had reached a suitable level. On another occasion after getting to bed we found that we were in a paddock inhabited by horses. Some of them came sniffing round our windows. But that, we felt, though interesting, did not rate moving the van. And all our minor troubles did not affect the fact that the van solved many of our problems. All in all, St Patrick's Van was just what was needed in the Minnipa Mission.

I have no doubt that the good people in Ireland who gave the van were thinking mostly of the way it could be used in pastoral ministry. And they were right. The van revolutionised the way I could work my parish. I could go about my parish visitations without worrying about where I was going to spend the night. It was wonderful to have a mobile bed! But, as I shall point out, it proved to have wider uses as the days went by.

But first we had to get it to Minnipa, and as the van was to be driven almost exclusively in South Australia it had to be registered in that state. The first stage of the journey was straightforward. The New South Wales traffic authorities gave me a permit to enable me to drive the unregistered vehicle to the N.S.W. border on my way to South Australia. I was pulled up by an alert traffic cop within 20 miles of starting the journey, but he was quite satisfied with the permit. And nobody seemed to take an interest after that.

When we reached Albury I went to the police station to get the necessary permission to drive further, but was told that they could not give me the permission to travel over Victorian roads. I must get that permit over the border.

So I went across to Wodonga, where I met one of the most obstructionist officials I can remember. I explained the position: I wanted to get to South Australia to register the vehicle there and I was asking permission to drive through Victoria to get there. 'You should have got that fixed up in New South Wales where you bought the vehicle' he said. I explained that the New South Wales officials had told me that they had no authority over Victorian roads, and that Victorian officials would see me through to South Australia. But he was adamant. I should have had it fixed in New South Wales.

On the face of it that was curious, implying that N.S.W officials have more control over Victorian roads than do Victorians! Perhaps the people at headquarters in Melbourne could help? I went off and telephoned the authorities in Melbourne, but the man on the other end of the line was evidently an underling, one who did not know the answer to my problem and could not be bothered to find out. We got nowhere. It appeared that no authority in Victoria could (or would) allow me to travel through their state!

So it was back to Albury. There in the end the exasperated man in authority gave me a document reading as nearly as I can recall it: 'Owing to difficulties encountered in crossing Victoria, Permit no. so-and-so is hereby extended to enable the unregistered vehicle to be driven to South Australia.' He said, 'I am giving you permission to drive along the Murray until you reach the South Australian border, but if you like to go through Victoria I can't stop you. And on what they have said to you I don't see what they could do to you.'

Neither could I. So I drove through Victoria and nobody questioned me anywhere. Then when I got to Bordertown in South Australia I went to the local authorities and discovered that I could not register the van until I got it to Adelaide. But the man issued me with insurance, without which, he said, I could not drive on South Australian roads. I privately wondered whether the insurance on an unregistered vehicle would be valid, but that was what the man said so that was what I did. I drove on to Adelaide very carefully.

In Adelaide I drove to the building where registration was to be effected and breathed a sigh of relief. At long last all was OK. I registered the van, got number plates affixed and felt at peace with the world. But as I was driving along East Terrace a burly traffic cop waved me to the curb. He came over, leaned on the window alongside me and said, 'St Patrick's Van. St Patrick's Van.' 'That's right' I replied, 'St Patrick's Van.' 'Didn't I see St Patrick's Van this morning driving without number plates?' 'You may well have,' I said. 'I picked up the van in Sydney and could not register it until I got it here.' 'Did you have it insured?' he asked. 'I fixed that up in Bordertown' I said. He straightened himself up, said, 'I never saw you!' went back to the middle of the road and held up a double decker bus.

On the way to Minnipa we had a hot and dusty drive, punctuated at one stage with a mechanical problem. Fortunately, we were not far from Kimba and there a mechanic had a considerable search for the trouble, finally locating it in a piece of gauze choked with fluff just before the carburettor. Even new engines can give problems! But we made it to Minnipa without further mishap and prepared for the next round of visiting and services.

Just to have Mildred with me was an advantage. Women living

on farms can have a difficult life. I remember one saying to me, 'We get tired of seeing nothing but men!' Another put the same thought this way: 'I get sick of the sight of trousers. On the farm there are only men to do the work and when a car drives up – out walks another pair of trousers!' So when St Patrick's Van turned up and out walked a charming young lady in a dress, that was quite something for the women of the bush. There is a ministry to women that can be exercised only by a woman and it was good to have Mildred accompany me and from time to time go off for a secret session with the lady of the house.

My wife is a triple certificated nurse and we found that that made her a very important person. In the Minnipa Mission area there was a small hospital at Wudinna (about 20 miles south of Minnipa) and Dr Trudinger had his residence in that town. But there were no other medical facilities throughout our area. We found that people tended not to go to Wudinna if they could avoid it, though not because they did not care for the medical facilities there. On the contrary they valued them highly. But Wudinna seemed a long way away, petrol cost money and anyway was rationed, and it was better to stay at home if possible. They did what they could and only sought the doctor's help if it was unavoidable.

Tom Jones decided that we should make the most of Mildred's medical expertise, so he supplied some medical equipment which we could take with us as we travelled round in the van. It helped our medical ministry. Thus one day as we visited, the lady of the house mentioned that she had 'a sore finger.' When Mildred looked at it she found that there had been an original prick caused by a thorn. The thorn had not been removed and the little wound had turned septic. The finger had swollen to twice its normal size, the whole hand was now swollen and the arm was beginning to be affected. Why did the woman not seek medical help? Well she lived 30 miles away from the doctor and petrol was scarce. These were days of petrol rationing and nobody did any travel that was not essential. However, in this case Sister Morris was able to effect repairs and prescribe further treatment, with the result that after a little time things returned to normal for the lady.

Then there was the man who hit his finger with a hammer, causing damage but not breaking the skin. After a few days he could not stand the pain any longer, so he took his pocket knife and slit his finger to let some blood out and obtain a measure of relief. When we arrived he horrified the nurse, used as she was to sterilised scalpels rather than not-too-clean pocket knives for such jobs. 'They're tough, mighty tough in the west!' But the farmer had apparently done no great damage and there was nothing that Sister could add to the treatment.

On another occasion we paid a pastoral visit to a farmer and his wife. We had a leisurely chat over afternoon tea. Then, just as we were about to leave, the farmer's wife said to Mildred, 'I wish you'd have a look at my boy. He's not well.' Mildred was glad to do this, but when she did she exclaimed, 'I think this boy has acute appendicitis. If you don't get him to a doctor straight away, I can't answer for the consequences.' It happened that this was in the northern part of our area and the nearest doctor and hospital were on the coast at Streaky Bay. The farmer could drive his son there just as easily as we could (and perhaps faster!). So we left them to it and got out of the way. We learned later that they made a quick trip to Streaky and that the op. was quite successful.

I recall an occasion when we got home from a week's trip among the farms somewhat tired from our journey. The farmers like to stay up talking to us when we visit. They see us only now and then, so they make the most of the opportunity to talk. Then in the morning farm work demands that we all get up early for breakfast. It's all right for our hosts – they only have it one night. But we found that it begins to tell on us, especially with travelling all day in addition. Anyway, on this occasion the somewhat tired travellers had just begun to think of tea when a casualty arrived. It was a matter of a broken arm, which Sister dealt with capably, taking advantage of the opportunity to further my education as junior (very junior, I fear!).

Then there was the problem of a baby who was perpetually cranky. Mildred talked with the parents and found that they were overfeeding the child. She pointed out that a baby's tummy can take just so much, and she added that if they kept on feeding it the way they were the child might well die. 'She may as well die with a full tummy as an empty one' said the farmer. Fortunately, his wife took a much more realistic view of the situation and gratefully accepted Mildred's suggestions for a diet. Next time we were there the baby was thriving.

There was one occasion when I had been on one of my long trips and Mildred had stayed home. The night I got back I turned wearily into bed, but before I could get to sleep there was a loud knocking at our front door. I got up quickly, but before I could get to the door and open it somebody else came to the back door and finding it unlocked barged straight in. 'There's a baby on the way,' an agitated man explained, 'and we can't get to Wudinna in time!'

Sister Morris decided that my study was to be the delivery room. Speedily we cleared the furniture out of the way and put the sponge rubber mattress from the van on the floor. I was instructed to boil water and to get quantities of newspaper. Indeed, so insistent was the demand that from that night on I have been convinced that gallons of boiling water and reams of newspaper are the prime necessities for handling a birth! We got the pregnant lady into my study and between her and Mildred all that was necessary was done. In just 20 minutes from the time the hammering on our door occurred the new mother was able to call out to her own mother, 'It's a girl, Mum!' We were all more than pleased that there had been no complications.

Mildred maintained that the most important part of her work was among the babies. Nearly all the mothers lived a long way away from the doctor and in the Minnipa area the word 'clinic' was, of course, a word without meaning. When problems arose about feeding the baby they had to be solved without outside help and most of the farmers' wives, though very caring, were not skilled in drawing up diets for infants. Then there were childish ailments which had a habit of making their appearance. So Mildred found herself in constant demand. It was not often that bush mothers had a triple certificated nurse call on them in their homes! And when there was no real ailment or anything specific going wrong Mildred found a frequent task was simply that of calming mothers' fears.

In Minnipa itself some of the ladies made use of Mildred's talents by having her appointed lecturer to their V.A.D. classes. In due course a number of them sat for an examination in first aid and we were all very pleased when the pass rate was 100 per cent.

We were sitting down to tea one evening when a lady popped in to see us accompanied by a little girl who had an abscess on one ear. The mum explained that she had just seen Dr Trudinger on one of his visits to our town and that he had sent her round to us. He himself would shortly join the party and do some incising. We liked the thought that he could go ahead with a plan like this without the formality of informing us – there was a measure of trust in our little community. But we would have welcomed a little more notice.

So we left our meal and there was quite a scatter as we proceeded to turn my study into an operating theatre. (We kept on calling it my 'study', but the room in question has featured as Mildred's consulting room, an emergency dining room, a fellowship room, a committee room, a music room, and as I have mentioned earlier, one never-to-be forgotten occasion in the middle of the night, as a maternity ward. Still, I suppose the name's a good one because if no one else was using it I was allowed to read a book in it!) Anyway, in due course the doctor turned up and with Mildred to give the anaesthetic he did his stuff, firstly on the little girl and then on the local butcher whom he had picked up for some minor surgery as he went on his rounds.

Before he was through, however, news arrived that a farmer 15 miles away had had a bad accident and help was needed. While the doctor and Mildred did what was needed for the butcher, I prepared St Patrick's Van for its role as ambulance. That meant principally filling the tank with petrol, seeing that the sponge rubber mattress was in place in the back, and picking up the local Red Cross stretcher. The doctor added to the occasion by breaking into the Red Cross's cupboard to purloin splints, towels, and so on and we were on our way.

We found the patient in no good state. He had been working on a stripper, a fairly heavy machine for harvesting a crop. Somehow, he got in front of it and was run over when the horses for some reason took fright and bolted. He lived alone and there was no one to miss him, so he lay there in the paddock all through the afternoon in the hot sun.

A neighbour passing along the road at the end of the day saw his team of horses with the stripper attached caught up in the fence, so went to see why that had happened. The man was too badly injured to be moved in the normal way, so his discoverer went off for help. He telephoned the Wudinna hospital and the people there passed the word on to us. The man went back to the scene of the accident with some friends. They took with them a door which they had taken off some building and which was the best substitute they could think of for a stretcher. They put some bags containing chaff on the back of a truck, placed the door with the patient on it on the chaff and set off on the 36 miles to the hospital. They had gone about a mile when St Patrick turned up while Dr Trudinger was on the spot shortly afterwards, approximately six and a half hours after the accident.

When the doctor had done what he could there on the road we placed the patient on the stretcher, transferred him to the van and set out on the 35 miles to the hospital. The first part of the road (a back road) was in bad condition and every little jolt seemed to cause untold agonies for our patient. I was profoundly thankful when we reached a military highway, one of the few roads that were given attention in that part of the world and which accordingly had far less in the way of bumps and ruts than any other road in those parts.

We were able to get to the hospital all right, but then there was a wait for the doctor. His car had broken down somewhere along the way! Still he turned up in due course and made his patient as comfortable as he could for the night. When the full score of the patient's injuries was out we found that he had three broken ribs, a couple of breaks in his collar bones, a dislocated hip and a fair dose of shock. We were glad to have been of help. We thankfully disposed of a 'cuppa' with the hospital staff and set sail for home, where we arrived at around 2 am. But that was life in the bush in those days.

There were sometimes problems of diagnoses. A little girl came to our front door one day bringing tidings of a sick lady who, the child said, badly needed Sister Morris. The kid did not seem to know exactly what was wrong, but she was insistent that Sister Morris was urgently required. I concluded that the only thing to do was to go looking for my wife. It was a Saturday and on Saturdays in Minnipa Mildred was certainly busy. She always had a few injections as farmers' wives took advantage of the fact that their husbands were drilling with the Volunteer Defence Corps and hitched a ride into the town to get their ailments attended to by Sister. In addition, she lectured the Red Cross Detachment and then conducted the young ladies of the district in a Country Women's Association choir.

On this occasion she arrived back home from the choir just in time to stop me going on a voyage of exploration to find out precisely where she was. She gathered up her tools of trade and we went off with the little girl. At the farmhouse, Sister had a session with her patient after which she decided to telephone the doctor. The people had no phone, so that meant going to the nearest neighbour who had one. Fortunately, this was only a mile or so away (though with four gates to pass through). The trouble was that Dr Trudinger could not be found; like the parson, he had a huge area to cover and on this occasion nobody knew where he was. Instead Mildred discussed the case with the matron of the hospital, left a full list of symptoms for the doctor to peruse when found, and went back to the patient to await developments.

When we got back to the patient, we found that her condition had continued to deteriorate. After a time, Mildred decided that we must take her to the hospital. So, St Patrick's Van became an ambulance again. Mildred stayed in the back with the patient and I had the husband with me in front. We began with a badly rutted road, but after we reached the military highway it was easier.

Our troubles were largely over when we reached the hospital, but those of the matron weren't. The hospital was full; every bed was occupied. One of her nurses was off duty on the sick list, she had no sister to help her and no domestic staff at all. But the matron of a country hospital is not easily defeated and quite soon she had our patient installed in a bed in a corridor. She sent us on our way assuring us that the patient would be quite all right. So we said our farewells and went back home, listening to the sick one's husband reminiscing on earlier days and congratulating BCA on the wisdom of sending out a vehicle like St Patrick's Van. That concluded our connection with the case, but we were glad to hear later that the patient had recovered.

Mildred was kept busy at around that time with injections for whooping cough and for diphtheria. The rectory was an interesting sight on days announced as injection days. Children of assorted sizes and ages turned up, some obviously fearful, some full of bravado, some curious, and one or two who looked forward to acquiring the hero status of those who had endured the needle! One young hopeful announced his ambition of having a hundred injections before he was through! Some made sure that Mum was there to see them through their hour of trial, while others scorned any aid. Mostly they went through the ordeal unflinchingly, though some gave tongue in no uncertain manner. One little sufferer confided in his mother when he went home, 'Mrs Morris stuck a pin in me!' He was broken hearted. He knew Mrs Morris and had not thought she would do such a thing to a little boy!

Tom Jones had been instrumental in getting St Patrick's Van assigned to Minnipa and it was fitting that on one occasion when he was visiting us he saw something of its use. A lady in Minnipa had had all her teeth out, and when she was bleeding badly they called Sister Morris in to help. Mildred did what she could, then telephoned the doctor at Wudinna. He came up to see the patient and then said she must go to hospital. So at around 11.30 pm I drove Sister and patient to the hospital and the safety of expert medical help. Tom was impressed and wrote about it in *The Real Australian*.

I have mentioned some of Sister Morris's exploits in connection with St Patrick's Van. But, of course, people did not get sick only when the van was at home and available. There was one notable occasion when I was away on a trip and Mildred was at home. A very sick man turned up and it was necessary to get him to hospital and doctor as quickly as it could be done. On this occasion the Roman Catholic priest turned ambulance driver and made for the hospital in his car at top speed, while the delirious patient in the back seat laid out Japanese in the white snow. In due course they all reached hospital safely and the last I heard the patient was progressing satisfactorily.

Mildred telephoned to call me back from one trip to convey vey a gentleman to hospital. He had an acute back problem and travelling in a car meant a great deal of pain. Failing St Patrick's Van, he would have had to travel on the back of a farm buckboard. However, with the combined efforts of Sister Morris and the sponge rubber mattress in the back of the van we got him to hospital in comparative comfort.

Local people came to take quite a proprietorial interest in St Patrick's Van, and they followed our various trips with some eagerness. I was interested to find out that when Dr Trudinger was confronted with a emergency anywhere in our general area he had come to ask, 'Where is the van?'

The van had other uses than getting us to the sick and to church services and to providing comfortable sleeping quarters. Mildred learned to drive and on many of our trips she drove while I continued my studies. I very much wanted to secure the University of London's degree of Bachelor of Divinity (which could be taken anywhere in the world if the local education authorities agreed to supervise the examination), but my parish did not give me much time to sit quietly reading. But with many miles of travelling I had quite a lot of time I could read while my capable spouse looked after the problems of getting us to wherever we were going. I guess a car would have done this part of the job quite well, but the van was much more comfortable than the De Soto it replaced.

I have told of some occasions when St Patrick's Van was used as an ambulance. But on one occasion it had the very different function of being a hearse. One of our Minnipa parishioners was taken ill and admitted to the Wudinna hospital. But she did not recover. Her family, of course, wanted her to be buried in the Minnipa cemetery. So I drove the van to Wudinna and brought the body back for burial.

There was a sequel to that. The lady and her family had been very active members of our church, so there was wide interest in them. But they did not have relations anywhere nearby and there was the problem of what to do with the children. There was a boy who stayed on the farm with his father, but there were two girls aged 16 and 14. In the end, after all the options had been canvassed, it was agreed that they should come and live with us at the rectory. So from then on Mildred's travels were limited for a year or two until other arrangements took over. It was interesting for a newly married couple to have an instant family of this kind! But they were fine girls and we were glad to have them.

That Mildred's work was widely appreciated was brought home to us in a letter she received. It was on stationery headed 'Central Eyre Peninsula Hospital (Inc.), Wudinna, via Port Lincoln' and it read as follows:

Dear Sister,

I have been requested by the 'Board of Management' of the above hospital, the 'District Council' and the 'Local Board of Health' to say Thank you! for your ready assistance among the sick of the district.

So many deeds of kindness are often performed by a nursing sister which are unnoticed by the general public, but I feel sure you will accept this letter as a mark of appreciation for your valued work in this district.

On behalf of the members of the above institution I would again say Thank you, and would ask that you accept my personal good wishes.

Yours sincerely,

J.B.S. Whitehead District Clerk and Secretary.

Then there was a paragraph or two in *The West Coast Sentinel*, a newspaper published in Streaky Bay and which had a wide circulation throughout our region. Headed 'Valuable Work of Mrs Morris', it read,

Minnipa has cause to be thankful to Mrs Morris, wife of the Rev. Morris. A triple certificated sister, she has had a wide experience in all branches of nursing and baby welfare work. During the recent epidemic around

77

Minnipa of gastroenteritis, she was sought by many in the district. While she at all times keeps in the closest touch with Dr Trudinger, she is on the spot, whereas he is 25 miles away.

Mrs Morris does not seem to mind the calls made on her, and is ever ready to assist anyone who needs her, be it at any hour of the day or night.

Apart from helping her husband in his church work, tending the sick, and mothering two motherless girls, she finds time to give home nursing and first aid lectures at Yaninee and Minnipa and to train the local CWA younger set choir. Being a trained singer and accomplished pianist, Mrs Morris' tuition has wrought pleasing progress, as was evidenced by their singing at the concert last Saturday night.

6

Station Country

I have explained that my parish was made up of quite number of farming districts. To the east and the north of my area the rainfall was not quite as abundant and we soon passed out of farm country to an area where crops could not grow but where sheep did very well. There was abundance of salt bush and blue bush and the sheep stations flourished.

There came a day when the Reverend Tom Jones decided that I ought to go through the area and provide spiritual ministrations to the station dwellers. Tom pointed out that BCA had a nursing sister up at Tarcoola on the transcontinental railway line and he thought I should at least go as far as that. In the event I did this, and also went a bit further to Mount Eba and McDouall's Peak to the north of the transcontinental line. This added a huge area to my parish and an area very different from that of the farms I had been working among.

When I asked the Bishop of Willochra where the northern boundary of my parish would now be he looked at me in surprise. 'There's no one working north of you,' he said, 'Go as far as you can go!' This resulted in a parish totalling about 40,000 square miles according to my successor. I never stopped to work it out, though I rather think his calculation was a bit on the high side. But there was certainly plenty of room. I planned to visit the sheep stations once a quarter, but by the time I got to Mount Eba I was visiting some of them only once in six months. I felt that that was little enough and refused to take on any more. Less than twice a year was surely not very useful.

The sheep stations I now visited were, of course, much larger than the farms. Whereas with farms we talked in terms of acres, in the stations it was a matter of square miles. One of the stations now added to my area was 3,000 square miles in area (and ran 44,000 sheep), and most of the others were quite large (though Yarna was of only about 200 square miles, with about 7,000 sheep). And for the most part they were not used to visiting clergymen. At one station I was told I was the first member of the cloth they had seen in three years and previous to that there had been only occasional visits. This story was repeated over and over: apparently there had never been a regular ministry in the station country. The bishop visited some of the stations himself, but in the nature of the case his visits were few. He could not leave the affairs of his diocese for the time that would be needed for such visitations.

The people on the stations lived lonely lives. There was the little handful of people necessary to run the station, but apart from that, they saw practically nobody. Why would anyone want to go through those remote parts? It was terrible for the children, deprived as they were of the society of other children of their age.

I recall one station where there were two little boys. Towards the end of my visit their mother asked whether I had noticed anything about them. 'They're pretty quiet,' I said. To which she rejoined that they were better than they had been. At an earlier time on the rare occasions when a visitor arrived, in their shyness they would hide themselves under a bed! She and her husband had decided that they must send the lads to a boarding school, but they were dreading both the break with the little fellows and what being part of a schoolboy community would do to them. But what else could they do? Somehow the lads had to learn to live with people.

For the traveller, a continuing hazard was gates. It is, of course, important that gates be kept closed which meant a stop as we came to one, getting out and opening it, back into the van to drive through, out again to shut the gate, and finally back into the van to go on one's way. It is better if one is accompanied, for then the passenger can do what is needed. On one of my trips I was accompanied by the Rev. David Livingstone, the Rector of Streaky Bay, a friend of many years standing, and who had previously been the Rector of Wilcannia. He told me that on a trip through his parish when he was at Wilcannia he was once accompanied by a man who wanted to see something of the country. The passenger jokingly objected to opening all the gates, so David magnanimously agreed to open all over 300. Accordingly, they counted them and on the whole trip passed through 297 gates. I never counted the gates on my station trip (perhaps because I was never generous enough to open all over 300!). But there were certainly plenty.

At least the gates in the station country were usually solid and straightforward. In this they contrasted with many of the 'cockies' gates' in the farming land. These consisted of a number of strands of wire attached to a fence post at one end and to a piece of wood at the other. To close the 'gate' the bottom end of this piece of wood was placed in a loop of wire attached to a fence post and the top was kept in place by a stick attached to the fence post in such a way that one end of it could be placed behind the top of the wood that was the end of the 'gate' and the other attached by a loop of wire to the top strand of the 'gate'. This kind of 'gate' could serve very well, but opening such a contraption was not always straightforward. It was all too easy to lose one's grip on the stick at the top, in which case it was liable to swing back smartly and hit one in the chest, while the 'gate' collapsed in a tangle of wire on the ground. Mildred has never forgotten her first encounter with such a gate. It brought about a hatred of all cockies' gates!

One incident in David's trip sticks in my mind. As we were driving along, we saw a wriggling black line right across the road. 'Snake!' yelled David. I hastily stopped the car and we ran back to relieve the world of a monstrosity only to find that our 'snake' was a line of caterpillars!

I had not ceased to complain about the roads in my farming country. There was never enough money for the work that needed doing on them. But at least we all knew where the roads were and from time to time some maintenance was done on at least some of them. In the station country there was no attempt on the part of government (state or local) to keep up the roads. They were purely station property and if the owners of the stations wanted roads they must make them themselves. So I found some pretty rough tracks. There was one occasion in May when I travelled a road over which only four vehicles had been since Christmas! Such a road is practically indistinguishable from the countryside in places.

Some of these roads can be treacherous. A number of times I was on a track that crossed a salt lake. Now a salt lake can be a very welcome sight. As I have pointed out, the roads in those parts are universally bad and one jolts from bump to bump. But a salt lake is perfectly smooth and it gives an indescribable sense of peace and wellbeing when, after leaping from crag to crag on what is laughingly called a 'road', one drives across one. But there is the drawback that the salt lakes are in the low spots; they are that part of the landscape to which the drainage flows when there is any rain. If there is going to be any soft spot, it will be in the salt lake.

Mildred and I were driving across Lake Everard once when St Patrick's Van broke through the crust. Carefully I backed out and we were able to resume our journey. But we stuck again. And again. We were not far from completing the half mile crossing when St Patrick's back wheels went down badly. I had often stuck before in sand or mud, but a salt lake is different. It has a hard crust, but if you break through that crust it seems that the further you go down the sloppier things are.

In this case I did the wrong thing and left the track. You should never leave the track on a salt lake. The track is where it has been proved that you can get through. I had been put off by the fact that we had repeatedly bogged on the track, even if we had so far managed to get out each time. But the shore looked tantalisingly close, so I made for it. And, of course, broke through the crust again. This time there was no backing out. Or getting out in any other way that I could see. We did all the proper things. Let air out of the tyres to give a wider spread and thus more grip. Packed bushes under the wheels, again to give more grip. We tried everything but could not move the wretched van. In the end it was clear that we needed help if ever we were to get out.

So, I left Mildred to look after the lake while I had a stroll of fifteen-and-a-half miles to the nearest station home. I am not much of a hiker and I cannot say that I really enjoyed that stroll, especially the places where the track went through sand or went up hill. But in the end I made it to the Lake Everard homestead at around 4.30 pm. (we had stuck at around 10 am). The men were, of course, all out doing what sheep men do on a station. So we had to wait for them to come in and have their evening meal before we could start. It was around 8.30 pm before we got to the van, where Mildred had surely now qualified for the title, 'The Lady of the Lake!' And I can still recall that her first words were 'I'm tired!' This to me who had walked fifteen-and-a-half miles while she sat comfortably in the van!

Our rescuers tried to get the van out under its own steam but couldn't budge it. So in the end they dug a hole on the shore, stuck a post in it, anchored a winch to the post, attached a line to the van and, after an hour's hard work, pulled the van out of the hole she had made. Then of course the wheels gripped, and it was a wonderful feeling to drive out of the lake, just eleven-and-a-half hours after we went in.

Next day we struck the Kokatha sands. First there was a long stretch of fairly level, heavy sand, and this was followed by miles of sandhills. This meant approaching each hill as fast as we reasonably could, crawling up one side of the hill hoping fervently that the van wouldn't stick, a sickening shudder as it trembled near the summit, then accelerating down the other side to get up speed for the next sandhill. Perhaps the worst feature of it was the winding road. As likely or not there would be a sharp bend just where the sand was deepest and the hill steepest. This made driving a thrilling pastime – the driver is constantly wondering whether the van will overturn or run into a tree or just get stuck! As it happened on this trip, we had little trouble with the sand. The rain that had caused our trouble in Lake Everard had packed the sand down a bit and driving through it was not over difficult.

On other occasions in hot, dry weather the sandhills posed problems. Whenever I made that trip, I had to cross four stretches of sandhills each about seven miles in length. I had the ambition to complete the trip without ever being stuck in the sand, but never made it. At one time or another I went through each of those four stretches without getting stuck, but not all on the same trip. And on the other side of the ledger there was the time when I was stuck ten times in one day, taking three-and-a-half hours to get over the worst of the stretches of sandhills. There was one terrible place in the Kokatha sands called 'The Big Bend'. As the name indicates the road took a turn on the sandhill and it was very difficult to climb. Usually I got stuck and had to back out and try again. It took me several trips before I managed the feat on my first attempt.

There are not many places where the touring motorist can buy petrol in that country. I carried a couple of eight-gallon drums which helped get me through. And, especially where I met the older station families, there was a tradition that the station owner fills up the parson's petrol tank so that he can get to the next station in comfort. Where the station was owned by a large pastoral company who put in a manager such courtesies were rare. But it was a wonderful help where it was done.

On the occasion when the van got stuck in the salt lake we went on our way to Kokatha station and then on to Kingoonya, where I had arranged to have a service. But the delay in getting us out of the lake meant that we arrived a day late! Quite a congregation turned up, I was told (19 people!), and had to go away again. But most of them came back the next night and we were able to worship together. These little services in the outback meant a good deal. The congregations could not meet frequently (I got to Kingoonya only four times in a year), so they valued the opportunity of meeting with other people in the worship of God.

Once when I was in Kingoonya the *Tea and Sugar* arrived. This was the name given to a goods train with provision vans attached, including such things as a general stores van and a butcher's van. The procedure was to place an order at Port Augusta (where the train started), then pick up one's goods and pay for them when it reached one's own station. The country there is very flat and the first thing we saw was some smoke against the horizon. Then a tiny dot appeared which turned out to be the engine and in due course the whole train was visible. The whole town turned up at the railway station to pick up their supplies (and do a little gossiping!).

It was at Kingoonya that I made my acquaintance with bush cricket. A match was arranged between Kingoonya and the Post Master General's department. It was to start at 2 pm, but nothing happened until about 3 pm when a few enthusiasts began putting out the mats and having a bowl at one another. By 4 pm we were all set to start, but the ladies of the Country Women's Association announced that afternoon tea was ready so we all did our bit by what they served up. I found myself drafted into the P.M.G. team and we fielded first. Our skipper put on the only man he knew could bowl for the first over, then looked round the place for another bowler and I found myself drafted. Eventually we got them out for 98. A big difficulty was that every time a wicket fell, we had to get the new batsman out of the pub and that took time. When either team batted we had only two pairs of pads, so that when a wicket fell we had to wait for the pads to be transferred to the new batsman. When it was our turn to bat the captain called on Whelan, but he was already in the pub, so he substituted Rankin who was likewise occupied. That is why I found myself opening the batting.

After a few balls one hit me on the pads and there was an appeal for l.b.w. That is when we found out that we had no umpires! I never found out who won the game (if anyone!). But I do know why country publicans take a deep interest in cricket matches!

We went on to Tarcoola, where Sister Symons ran a little nursing hostel, from which she ministered to the medical needs of the town and to a big outback clientele. The flying doctor from Ceduna made visits from time to time which must have been a great help to her. She was a faithful soul and a hard worker. She had a great time with Mildred – I don't think their tongues stopped all the time we were there.

There was a service in the little church on Sunday. I was told that the Presbyterian, Methodist and Congregational churches had combined to set up the church and normally a minister from one of these churches was the minister for all denominations in Tarcoola. But all the time I was there there was no such resident minister, so each time I visited the town I held a service to which people from all denominations came. Congregations were not large, but in that remote place and without regular services that was not surprising. But there were some good contacts and I was able to talk to a number of people about the things of God.

On the return journey (by a different route in order to visit other stations) we again struck trouble in a salt lake. It looked worse, for instead of being near the bank when we stuck, we were right in the middle of the lake. We could claim that we had done the right thing and had stuck to the track, but that did not alter the fact that we were also stuck in the track! With dismal memories of last week, we set to work. I dug the soil from around the wheels and we packed a runway with leaves. We tried various ways of shifting the van. We both sat in the van hopefully and I drove, but nothing happened. So, I pushed and Mildred drove and then Mildred pushed and I drove. As she was pushing when the van came out, she firmly maintained that she pushed it out of the lake!

At a number of stations, we found our visit coinciding with shearing. It was a new world to me to discover what went on in the process of removing the wool from the sheep. I used to go through the whole process, speaking in turn to the men who did each piece of work. I recall one Koori shearer who was beautiful to watch; he never wasted a movement. I timed him as he shore one sheep and he completed it in two minutes (whistling to himself 'The old rugged cross'). One of his mates told me that in the last shed he once shore seven lambs in seven minutes. He was poetry in motion.

I was specially fascinated by the wool classing and spent a lot of time watching how it was done and talking with the classers as to why they put one fleece into one category and another into a different one. And I was grateful for their patience in dealing with the questions of an ignoramus.

They were all somewhat surprised to find a parson visiting them, but after they got over the initial shock and decided that I was human they gave me the warmest of welcomes. There was often a church service. I was interested to discover that the important man was the union rep. It was no use talking to the owner or manager of the station or to anyone else in the visiting shearing team. The union rep. was the man who mattered. I would seek him out and ask whether the team would like a service in the evening. The reps. I met invariably agreed and we had some unusual services.

Those who attended came in their working clothes; they, of course, had no others with them. The service was always informal and subject to constant interruption as those who chose not to take part wandered in and out, by no means quietly. There was never an accompaniment, so I did not know whether to try some hymn singing or not. I had with me in the van a box of hymn books so there was no problem with the words. The music, of course, was quite another matter. I almost always began with 'Abide with me' for it is a well-known and well-loved hymn and I reasoned that if people don't know 'Abide with me' they don't know any hymn. I mostly took prayers from the *Book of Common Prayer*, and quite a few shearers and their mates had some recollection of these familiar passages and spoke to me appreciatively at hearing them again. I always had an attentive hearing as I preached the gospel message.

I recall one shearers' service where, just after I had concluded, the union rep. stood up and, as nearly as I can recollect it, said, 'I reckon it was pretty decent of Mr Morris to come all this way out 'ere to give us a service. And we ought to show 'im we appreciate it. And we're gonna. We're gonna take up a collection and 'ere's two bob to start it.'

With that he placed his two shillings on the table. I have never seen a congregation empty out so fast! I thought at first that there was some objection to giving financial aid to the church, but as the men drifted back to make their offering the true explanation dawned on me. Out there in the bush there's nothing to spend money on. So nobody had any money in their pockets when the collection was announced. They all went off to where they had their purses and the like and then came back to play their part in the most unusual collection I have ever seen.

On another occasion there was evidently a mix-up about the time. I came down to the shed after dinner at the station homestead, only to find a couple of poker schools at their flourishing best. But after a short time, they closed down and most of the poker players joined the congregation.

It was a privilege and a new experience for me to see the last stages of the breaking in of a horse. The owner approached the animal very slowly, speaking softly (which he did at every stage). At first, he did no more than pat the horse and rub it gently. Then came the putting on of a bridle and a saddle; a rope was put round the horse's neck and the animal was led slowly round the enclosure. To get it used to turning the bit was connected to the girth by a chain in such a way that the neck was bent a little. The man got away from the horse and urged it on so that it went round and round the enclosure. Eventually the man got on the horse's back very gingerly and almost immediately got off again. He did this a number of times until the horse got used to him and another rider did the same so that the animal could get used to more than one rider. After some time like this the gate was opened and horse and rider went off for a little trip. All this is doubtless commonplace to those used to horse riding. But for a city slicker let loose in the country it was fascinating.

One of my ports of call was Glenloth. In an earlier day it had evidently been a flourishing goldfield, but the precious metal petered out and when I visited it there were only three families left. They welcomed the suggestion of a service and we held it in one of the homes, as far as I know the first ever to be held on that goldfield. It was a quiet little service, the surroundings were neither elaborate nor ecclesiastical, the singing perhaps would not have appealed to the music lover, but it was hearty, and the atmosphere was one of sincere worship. There we sought God, and in his love and mercy we found him. A unique feature was that we had 100 per cent of the local population – the whole 11 of them!

Doing the Tarcoola trip during the summer could be trying. I recall one such trip made during a heatwave. Tarcoola lies in a general northerly direction from Minnipa which meant that all the way up I had the sun shining through my windscreen. Those were before the days of air conditioning and I was nearly cooked by the time I arrived. With the hot weather the sand flows freely, so it is not surprising that I stuck in the sandhills now and then. Digging oneself free in a heatwave is definitely not recommended. But I guess the important thing is that in the end

I made it!

And on Sunday the heat continued; it was the hottest day for ages. If there was a cool spot among all those iron and weather-board homes, I certainly did not find it and did not even hear about it. Now the Tarcoola church was never meant for services in heatwaves. It was a nice little building on the inside, but small and its outer walls were of corrugated iron. The Tarcoola folk either knew it too well to come out for a service or perhaps they were too prostrate to leave their homes. Anyway, we had ten people for service. A bush ministry is like that. You go hundreds of miles to take a service, struggling through heat and sand, and ten people turn up! And you wonder whether it's worthwhile and whether you weren't a fool to leave the comforts and conveniences of the city.

And the next day you have your answer. You call on a lonely boundary rider and his wife, you talk about the doings of the world near at hand and far away. You bring them up to date with the news for their radio has broken down. You talk with them about the love of God, you read to them from the gospel, the three of you join in discussing the passage, what it tells you about God and what it tells you about the way we should serve him. You recognise again the important of faith and of putting your whole trust in God. You join in prayer.

You go on your way rejoicing in the continuing heat and come to Glenloth again, where three families meet. Two of them have had to drive some miles in the heat and we worship in a little corrugated iron house without even a verandah to shield it from the worst of the burning heat. They come at the most awkward hour of 2 pm on Monday afternoon and you know it's all worthwhile. You realise that people still want to hear the message of Christ and of his atoning death, the only message that can save a person or a nation or a world torn by war. And you go on your way breathing a prayer of thankfulness for men like Sydney James Kirkby who saw the vision splendid and laboured to make possible the continuing outback work of BCA.

The roads could play curious tricks. There was one occasion when we went through the stations not long after rain when the ground was soft. I drove in the wheel ruts as was normal, but at one point there was a small tree stump left in the middle of the track when they cut it through a piece of scrub. The stump caught on something at the front of the van and the ground was soft enough for the van to drag the stump out of the soil and bring it forward a little.

Then as the van continued its progress the container that held the battery met the stump with the result that the battery cable and a battery terminal were forced up against the metal floor of the driver's compartment thus short circuiting the battery. We did not know exactly what had happened, but we did know that there were sparks flying and a sudden heating up of the floor. There was an immediate halt and a speedy evacuation of the van! When I examined the floor to discover the extent of the damage, I found that the part of the cable that was in touch with the floor had burned out completely. But fortunately, it left enough of the rest of the cable to make the necessary connection. Had the whole width of the cable burned out or had it run the battery completely flat we would have been in some trouble. We were on a stretch of about 70 miles without inhabitant and our mishap occurred somewhere about the middle.

On another occasion I was told of an old track, seldom used, which would take quite a few miles off a journey I was making. But I found that it had never been used very much and certainly not for a long time before I tried to follow it. In many places it was hard to see where the track was. Now and then I had to stop the van and cast about on foot until I found it again! Fortunately, it did not go lost for great lengths and in the end I made it.

Travel in such country is hard on the vehicle. I never did the stations trip without the van needing garage attention at the conclusion.

People on the stations were invariably welcoming. For the most part they seemed to have some church connections but whatever their church they welcomed me. I found one Roman Catholic manager and his family who asked me to conduct a service in their home each time I came through that area. This was not invariable, but it mostly happened.

A bonus in the springtime was the vast quantity of wildflowers. In our farming country we never saw many of them, but out in the Ranges the wildflowers were everywhere. There seemed to be thousands of acres of flowers quite uninterrupted by signs of civilisation.

There were some sad happenings. I recall visiting a sheep station in a very remote spot where I found the manager and his family grieving over the death of a little boy still in his infancy. There had been no clergyman to take a burial service, but they dug a grave not far from the station homestead and buried him there. Then when I next came to them, they asked me to read the burial service over the grave. It was a privilege to minister to the little family in their grief.

Indeed, I have always counted it a privilege to have been permitted to minister to people in the outback. Their lives were invariably lonely and their work was hard. But they were fine and welcoming people, and they did not take it amiss that a city-ite had come to be their minister. They never mocked at my ignorance of things rural, but they did their best to make farming and station life intelligible to me. And while for years I never had a congregation of any size I did have little groups of devout people, people who were glad to have the opportunity of joining in worship.

It was part of the duties of Tom Jones to visit the various areas serviced by BCA and on one of his visits to Minnipa he accompanied me on a trip through the station country. It was a great privilege to have him with me day and night for a couple of weeks and to have his comments on a wide variety of subjects. He gave an account of our trip in *The Real Australian* and summed it up in these words:

> I came home tremendously impressed with the worthwhileness of B.C.A. work. Before going on the trip I

had sometimes wondered if the great expense of such trips as these, and the sacrifices demanded of the missioner, were justified in such times as these.

But now I am absolutely convinced that B.C.A. is doing the right thing in carrying on. The sincere welcome given at each home and town, the times of prayer with lonely families miles away from any other habitation, the many expressions of blessing received through the services, the earnestness evident, and the eagerness with which the missioner was requested to 'come again and hold another service' – all were profoundly moving. B.C.A. is doing a grand job!

Epilogue

The Postmaster at Minnipa was in the habit of cooperating with me as I journeyed round the countryside by forwarding my mail to places where he knew I would be. So it was that one day, some five years after I began my work in the Minnipa Mission, I picked up my mail at Poochera and found in it a letter from Bishop Baker, the Principal of Ridley College, Melbourne.

The good bishop tentatively raised the question of the Vice Principalship of Ridley. The college had never had a Vice Principal but was thinking of appointing one. I rather think that for the most part they had never thought of me, either. I was certainly not widely known, and I doubted whether Minnipa was such a household name in Melbourne that its Rector would automatically become known there.

But somehow the connection had been made. Bishop Baker briefly outlined what the position would entail and suggested that I go over to Melbourne to talk to him and others so that they could see whether I would suit the position and I could see whether I wanted to work with them.

This came as a complete surprise to me. I had heard of Ridley College, but had never had anything to do with it. I knew nothing of the people there or of the way in which the college was run.

But obviously the invitation was one that had to be taken with full seriousness. So, in due course I made the journey to Melbourne. I had some good conversations with Bishop Baker and others. Questions were raised and discussions were held. There is no point in discussing them in detail here. The main thing is that in the end it was agreed that I would be the Vice Principal of Ridley.

This meant an exit from the Minnipa Mission in a rather unexpected way. It had been a wonderful five years. To live in the middle of a farming district together with quite a slice of station country was an unforgettable experience. I have always been grateful for the warmth of the welcome I received there, for the readiness of those country people to cooperate in setting forward the work of the kingdom of God and for what they taught me in so many areas of life.

My time at the Minnipa Mission proved to be the one opportunity I would have of close acquaintance with country life in a fairly remote region of Australia. Once I went to Ridley the rest of my professional life has been in academic circles. But those farmers and station hands put me very much in their debt and I have always been grateful for the opportunity of working among them. They gave me an insight into an important aspect of Australian life, an aspect that I had not previously been able to experience. And they have given me memories that I have cherished throughout the whole of my subsequent life.

This little book then is my tribute to the big-hearted people I met in the outback, whether on farms or on stations or in little country towns. I want to acknowledge my debt to so many battlers in their very difficult but important situations. And with them I want to link those in our cities who are interested enough in what is done in this vast country to support with their prayers and their gifts those who go out to minister to their outback cousins. I am indebted to both.

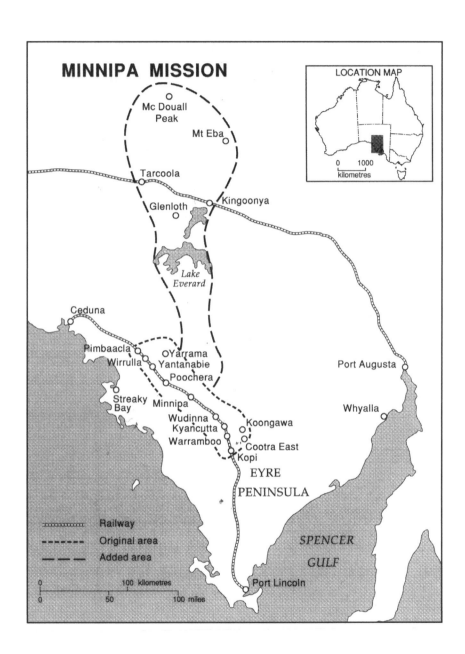

MINNIPA MISSION

LOCATION MAP

0   1000
kilometres

Mc Douall Peak

Mt Eba

Tarcoola

Glenloth

Kingoonya

Lake Everard

Ceduna

Pimbaacla

Wirrulla

Yarrama

Yantanabie

Poochera

Port Augusta

Streaky Bay

Minnipa

Wudinna

Kyancutta

Warramboo

Koongawa

Cootra East

Kopi

EYRE

PENINSULA

Whyalla

Railway

Original area

Added area

SPENCER

GULF

100 kilometres

0   50   100 miles

Port Lincoln

101

Appendix 1

Leon Morris' application for service, Bush Church Aid, 1938 (BCA Archives).

For

BUSH CHURCH AID SOCIETY

For Australia and Tasmania

QUESTIONS FOR CANDIDATES

It is a fundamental principle of the B.C.A. Society to support spiritual agents for spiritual work, and it is of essential importance that every Candidate should himself know and love the Lord Jesus Christ as his Saviour, and should have weighed well his responsibility before God, and have prayerfully sought his guidance before offering himself for any high and holy calling in the Church.

Candidates are requested to fill in answers to the following questions in the allotted spaces, and to return the paper to the Organising Missioner, Bush Church Aid Society, Diocesan Church House, George Street, Sydney, N.S.W.

Victorian Office: St. Paul's Cathedral Buildings, Flinders Lane, Melbourne.

1. Please give (a) your full name and address ... *Leon Lamb Morris 20 Premier St. Marrickville*

    (b) Date and place of birth ... *15·3·14 Lithgow*

    (c) Date and place of baptism ... *26·4·14 St. Paul's Lithgow*

    (d) Date and place of confirmation ... *6·5·28 St. Paul's Lithgow*

    (e) If in Orders, date of Ordination as Deacon and Priest ... *Deacon 13·2·38*

*2. (a) What leads you to believe that your own heart is under the influence of the Holy Spirit?   *See separate sheets*

    (b) What do you think of Christ and His Work on the Cross?

    (c) What do you understand by "personal salvation," and how is it obtained?

3. (a) Have you been confirmed, and how long have you been a regular Communicant of the Church of England?   *1 (a) Regular communicant since 13·5·28*

    (b) If you have ever been a member of any other Denomination, please say what it was and why you left it

    (c) What Parish Church do you now attend?   *St. John's Campsie (from 16·3·38)*

    (d) State briefly your reasons for being a member of the Church of England ... *Environment & conviction that C.of E. satisfies my spiritual needs more than any other I know.*

4. (a) How and where were you educated? ... *Lithgow Inter High; University of Sydney; Aust. Coll. Theol.*

    (b) If at school and college, please give names, and what degrees or diplomas you have taken ... *B.Sc. (Univ. of Sydney) Th.L. (Aust. Coll. of Theology)*

5. (a) What has hitherto been your occupation? .. *Schoolteacher*

    (b) In what are you at present engaged? ... *About to become curate St. John's Campsie*

    (c) Are your parents living? If so, where? ... *Yes 20 Premier St. Marrickville*

6. (a) Is any relative dependent upon you for support, wholly or in part, or likely to become so?   *Parents & brother partly dependent.*

    (b) If accepted for training, can you or your friends undertake the cost of such training or part thereof?

*(2) Candidates may fill in answers to this section on separate sheets of paper.

7. (a) Are you under any engagement, expressed or implied, with a view to marriage? ... ...   *No*

    (b) Are you a total abstainer? ... ...   *Yes*

8. (a) What is the state of your health? ... ...   *Good*

    (d) Are you aware of any bodily ailments? ...   *No*

    (c) What are your recreations and amusements, public and private? ... ...   *Reading; tennis*

    (d) Of what class of books, and of what periodicals has your general reading chiefly consisted? ...   *Text books for exams.*

    (e) What theological works have you read, and which of them has influenced you most? ...   *Books set for Th. L.*

9. (a) Is it your present purpose, if God permit, to make service in some ministry of the Church your life work? ...   *Yes*

    (b) If you think you have been specially called to any particular department of work, specify it ... ...   *—*

    (c) Would you, nevertheless, be willing to go to another field or department of work if the Committee thought it desirable? ... ...   *Yes*

    (d) If you feel it necessary to attach any condition to your offer, please specify it ... ...   *None*

    (e) What have you done specially to prepare yourself for such work? ... ...   *Studied for ordination*

    (f) Have you ever offered your services to any Bishop or to any other Missionary Society? If so, with what result? ...   *No.*

    (g) Kindly state what reasons have weighed with you in offering your services to this Society in particular ...   *I feel that the Lord has called me to serve with B.C.A*

    (h) Are you prepared to work loyally with your Bishop and with the Society? ... ...   *Yes*

10. (a) What Church work have you done? Please give details   *Lay reader all Saints Leichhardt, St. John's Warren S. School teaching etc.*

    (b) Are you able to ride, drive and groom a horse? Do you know anything of motor cycling and motor driving? Have you had any experience in the use of tools? ...   *No. No. No.*

11. Give the names and addresses of two clergy and of two laymen who are well acquainted with you, and to whom the Society may refer ... ...   *Separate sheet*

Candidates for training are accepted subject to satisfactory completion of their course. No B.C.A. Candidate should contract any matrimonial engagement during course of training.

SIGNATURE   *L. Morris*

PRESENT ADDRESS   *20 Premier St. Marrickville*

PERMANENT HOME ADDRESS   *20 Premier St. Marrickville*

DATE   *15 . 3 . 38*

2. (a) I believe that my heart is under the influence of the Holy Spirit firstly because I have been born again and know what it is to have old things pass away & all things become new. "If any man have not the Spirit of Christ he is none of his."

secondly, God's Word is sure & definite in promising the guidance of the Spirit to God's children.

Thirdly, I feel within me the Spirit's guidance.

(b) Briefly Christ is Perfect God and Perfect man. He is the only One who could make atonement for the sins of the world, which Work He accomplished by His death on Calvary.   John , 29

(c) "Personal salvation" is the removal of the sins of the individual through the Blood of the Lamb whereby the individual is justified in God's sight and saved from the punishment he had incurred by his sin.

It is obtained when the individual in simple faith accepts Christ as his Saviour and is "born of the Spirit"

Appendix 2

Letter from Leon Morris to Bush Church Aid requesting permission to marry, 1940 (BCA Archives).

Ans Feb 14
no assurance
given [?]

20 Premier St.
Marrickville

12. 2. 40

Dear Mr. Jones,

I have been thinking over a few preliminary arrangements preparatory to my entering service with B.C.A. and the question of marriage has cropped up. I write then to ask that I may be given a definite assurance that after a year's service as a single man the Society will be prepared to make such arrangements that my marriage may then take place.

Yours in the Master's service

L. Morris

Appendix 3

Article from a local newspaper, *The West Coast Sentinel*,
'Valuable work of Mildred Morris', no date
(Leon and Mildred Morris archives, Ridley College).

VALUABLE WORK OF MRS. MORRIS

Minnipa has cause to be thankful to Mrs. Morris. wife of the Rev. Morris. A triple certificated sister, she has had a wide experience in all branches of nursing and baby welfare work. During the recent epidemic around Minnipa of gastro enteritis, she was sought by many in the district. While she at all times keeps in the closest touch with Dr. Trudinger, she is on the spot, whereas he is 25 miles away.

Mrs. Morris does not seem to mind the calls made on her, and is ever ready to assist anyone who needs her, be it at any hour of the day or night.

Apart from helping her husband in his church work, tending the sick, and mothering two motherless girls, she finds time to give home nursing and first aid lectures at Yaninee and Minnipa and to train the local CWA younger set choir. Being a trained singer and accomplished pianist, Mrs. Morris' tuition has wrought pleasing progress, as was evidenced by their singing at the concert last Saturday night.

PERSONAL

Appendix 4

Letter of thanks to Sister Morris from the Secretary, Central Eyre Peninsula
Hospital, no date
(Leon and Mildred Morris archives, Ridley College).

Central Eyre Peninsula Hospital (Inc)

Wudinna
Via Port Lincoln

Sister Morris
Minnipa S.A.
Dear Sister

I have been requested by the "Board of Management" of the above hospital, the "District Council" & the "Local Board of Health" to say thank you! for your ready assistance among the sick of the District

So many deeds of kindness are often performed by a nursing sister which are unnoticed by the general public, but I feel sure you will accept this letter as a mark of appreciation for your valued work in this district

On behalf of the members of the above institutions I would again say Thank you, & would ask that you accept my personal good wishes

yours sincerely
J. W. S. Whitehead
District Clerk &
Secretary.

Appendix 5

Theologian left a legacy of faith and biblical text

THEOLOGICAL SCHOLAR
15-3-1914 – 24-7-2006

Leon Morris, perhaps Australia's most prolific biblical and theological author, has died, aged 92, at Karana nursing home in Kew after a fall that led to an infection and pneumonia.

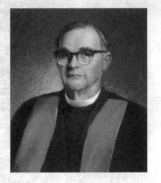

Morris, who was suffering from Alzheimer's, wrote more than 50 books of theology and biblical commentary that have sold nearly 2 million copies worldwide and been translated into many languages - an astonishing output for an Australian writing technical or academic books.

Morris was well known throughout the Christian world as a careful, conservative biblical scholar. Extraordinarily, he received no formal theological education, apart from two years of supervision for his doctorate in Cambridge. A self-taught theologian, he brought his rigorous and disciplined training in scientific inquiry to his study of the Bible and theology.

Morris was born in Lithgow, the first of five children of an iron founder. He began training as a teacher in 1931, with a degree in science. In his first year he was converted to Christ in the Anglican parish of Leichardt. At the Katoomba convention the next year he felt the call to ordained ministry.

Having qualified as a science teacher, he was required to serve out the five years of his bond to the Department of Education. However, while he worked as a teacher, he studied in his spare time for a licentiate in theology and topped the Australian College of Theology list. The archbishop of Sydney Howard Mowll, paid out his bond to the Department of Education and he was ordained to a curacy in Campsie in 1938.

In 1940, under the auspices of the Bush Church Aid Association, he began five years as priest in charge of the vast Minnipa mission in outback South Australia during World War II. Mildred Dann, whom he married in 1941, would drive the bumpy, dusty roads of South Australia while Morris studied New Testament Greek in the passenger seat.

He continued his private studies, gaining a bachelor of divinity from London University with first-class honours in 1943, and a master of theology in 1946. In 1945, he was invited to the position of vice-principal of Ridley College in Melbourne.

He spent 1950-51 in Cambridge gaining his PhD, which was later published as *The Apostolic Preaching of the Cross*, a book that became seminal for modern evangelical theology. He was encouraged in his study by professor (later archbishop) Michael Ramsay. In 1951 he became the first Australian elected to the Society for New Testament Studies.

In 1961, Morris accepted the position of warden at Tyndale House in Cambridge, a significant evangelical biblical research centre. Three years later, he courageously left this ideal academic post and returned to Ridley College as principal when the college was in severe difficulty, convicted that this was God's call to him.

During his 15 years as principal, he strengthened the college, gave it a worldwide reputation, built a new chapel and established it as an official residential college of Melbourne University, the first college to take both men and women. He was made a canon of St Paul's Cathedral in 1964 and a member of the university council in 1977. In 1966, he was runner-up in the election of the archbishop of Sydney.

During these years he continued his prolific writing, publishing commentaries on almost every book of the New Testament, many of which remain classics. He was in demand as a lecturer and preacher in Australia and overseas, where he was visiting professor at several colleges. He was famous for his dry with, conciseness, simplicity and attention to the detail of the biblical text applied relevantly.

He served on the boards of a number of Christian organisations, including the Evangelical Alliance, Scripture Union, Church Missionary Society and Bible Society, and he chaired the 1968 Billy Graham Crusade committee. As president of the Evangelical Alliance, he established TEAR fund, a significant Christian aid and development agency in Australia. He was a translator for the new international version of the New Testament.

In 1974, on his 60th birthday, he was presented with a festschrift from eminent biblical scholars from around the world.

In retirement, Morris continued writing from his large study in Doncaster. He lectured overseas several times and continued to preach regularly. He and Mildred were loyal members of Holy Trinity Doncaster, where he preached his final sermon late in 1997. Typically, he preached with few notes from the Greek text. As always, he was remarkably lucid. The Gospel of John held a place close to his heart and his magisterial commentary on John remains perhaps his magnum opus.

Morris was well known for his humble manner and gracious, Christian character. He leaves a vast legacy of theologically equipped ministers throughout the world upholding biblical Christian faith centered on the atoning death of Christ. His theology is the subject of a recently completed PhD in Queensland.

Mildred predeceased him in April 2003. They had no children. The Leon and Mildred Morris Foundation continues their generosity to many good causes. He is survived by his brother Max.

Obituary written by Peter Adam and Paul Barker, published in The Age,
15 August 2006.